J.K. LASSER'S

GUIDE TO TAX-DEFERRED INVESTMENTS

J.K. LASSER'S

GUIDE TO TAX-DEFERRED INVESTMENTS

Published by Simon & Schuster, Inc.
New York

Produced by Cloverdale Press, Inc.
133 Fifth Avenue
New York, New York 10003

Published by Simon and Schuster
A Division of Simon & Schuster, Inc.
Simon & Schuster Building
Rockefeller Center
1230 Avenue of the Americas
New York, New York 10020

Typography by Paragraphics
Manufactured in the United States of America

1 2 3 4 5 6 7 8 9 10

Library of Congress Catalog Number: 84-52736

ISBN: 0-671-55817-X

CONTENTS

INTRODUCTION

For centuries, mankind had to accept that two things in life, at least, were unavoidable: death and taxes. Along came the twentieth century. Death is still inevitable, but in the last couple of decades, man has concentrated with unprecedented ingenuity and determination upon the question of taxes...and the results have been extraordinary for the alert taxpayer, particularly if he or she has a good income. Taxes are still unavoidable, but they can be dramatically reduced, deferred for years, and otherwise manipulated for taxpayer benefit.

This book is for the taxpayer who wants an introduction to this changed, and continually changing, tax "opportunity." Thanks to recent revisions in U.S. tax law, almost every taxpayer has something to gain from an IRA (Individual Retirement Account) or Keogh plan; and in certain tax situations, an individual may also have good reason to invest in tax-deferred annuities or in bonds that have a tax-free yield.

The bulk of this book, however, deals with tax shelters, a mechanism for tax saving that has become something of a national phenomenon in the last couple of years. Is the tax shelter a gravy shelter or fool's gold? Is it a legitimate method of reducing one's tax obligation, or is it a swindle? The answers depend upon a number of factors, some of which are discussed in this book. Just because a certain tax shelter is printed in a brochure or recommended by a friend is no guarantee that it will work for you or will be accepted as legal by the Internal Revenue Service. To make sense for you, a tax shelter has to suit your specific income and tax situation. This book advisedly takes a cautionary view of shelters.

REDUCING YOUR TAXES: CAN YOU AFFORD IT?

Most forms of tax reduction operate for you by reducing the level of your *taxable income.* Therefore, your tax bill will be lowered because of the reduced amount of taxes you are obligated to pay.

Remember this simple rule for determining the value of a reduction in taxable income: Multiply the amount to be subtracted from your taxable income by the percentage of your tax bracket for the year. If, say, you are in the 30 percent tax bracket and enter a plan that will reduce your taxable income by $2,000, your actual saving will be $600 (30 percent of $2,000). In a lower tax bracket, the saving will be correspondingly less. The highest tax bracket today (about 50 percent) will save you in taxes approximately half of any amount you can subtract from your total taxable income.

The rule again: The amount you save is *not* the amount by which your taxable income is lowered; the amount you save is the percentage of your tax bracket multiplied by the amount to be subtracted from your taxable income.

The more you make, the higher your tax bracket; the higher your bracket, the more likely you are to benefit from techniques to lower your tax bill. Yet no matter what tax bracket you're in, if you look carefully at the proposals outlined in this book, you are likely to find a tax strategy that will be helpful. Just remember that legislation to encourage tax reduction was not enacted to give free rein to the citizen's desire to steal the government blind.

TAX SHELTERS: PLAY BY THE RULES

Despite what you might feel personally, the IRS does not subsidize greed. True, the most highly imaginative tax shelters can result in large tax savings for very wealthy investors. But it is equally true that the purpose of such tax shelters, from the government's point of view, is to encourage economic growth nationwide by making it more attractive for the taxpayer in a high tax bracket to invest in high-risk or economically useful programs, like exploration for oil or the building of low-income housing. Similarly, IRA or Keogh plans are thought to encourage individual savings and foster economic development by making larger amounts of capital available for expansion. In other words, behind every tax-savings plan discussed in this book is the hope that society will benefit in some way.

Understand, therefore, that the IRS looks upon every method of reducing your taxes as a cooperative venture, not an adversarial contest. In most cases, the IRS has made the rules crystal clear; you are expected to play by those rules. Don't try to "play the angles." As you will learn in chapter 3, the IRS is making an extraordinary effort these days to uncover questionable tax-saving schemes. The likelihood of getting caught is increasing almost daily, and the penalties are quite harsh.

Don't be one of those taxpayers who believes that a spare $5,000 or $10,000 in a good year is your ticket to the good life. With the right attitude, and with good, sound, long-term planning, you might be able to better your financial situation by taking advantage of legitimate opportunities to cut your annual tax liability.

Legitimate tax saving is not a get-rich-quick scheme. The way to get rich quick, as any tax adviser will tell you, is to increase your income. Tax-free, tax-deferred, and tax-sheltered income plans do not produce overnight bonanzas for the average American taxpayer. Sensibly entered into, they can often save you money, encourage stable financial planning, prepare you for the future, and, just as the law intends, contribute to the economic well-being of the nation. When you find your blood racing because of a rumor about the ease of making a killing with a tax shelter in, say, the leasing of jet airplanes, calm down and think. Remember the words of the American philosopher, P. T. Barnum: "There's a sucker born every minute." It's very unlikely that someone with a sure-fire, high-yield (and honest) tax deal is looking for *you.* When a deal sounds too good to be true, it probably is.

FINANCIAL CONSIDERATIONS

You can't save on taxes unless you are making money *and* investing it. That may sound obvious enough, but a surprising number of taxpayers miss one of the elements of this basic proposition.

There are tax shelters, for example, that make sense only for those in the highest income brackets. Others make sense only for the taxpayer with a relatively high income projected for a few years. For each plan discussed in this book you should examine your specific financial situation to determine applicability. In some situations, oddly enough, you can save so much on taxes that the savings backfire, subjecting you to the alternative minimum tax, or AMT (see page 40).

Keep in mind that saving taxes will require you to "salt away" or spend money. After that the plan you have chosen may become more abstract, and there may be talk of paper losses and paper gains; but first and foremost, you have to have the money to spend before you can reap the tax benefit. It follows, then, that you will judge any tax-saving plan in terms of your income and the amount of money you can comfortably spend (many tempting tax-saving schemes have a hidden sting, so when you invest in a plan, *never* use money that might be needed for day-to-day living).

You will most likely need expert advice when it comes to saving taxes—you certainly will if you decide to enter the world of tax shelters. Whether tax lawyer, accountant, or tax consultant, your adviser should be up to date on the most recent tax legislation and tax court rulings, able to examine your financial situation objectively, and ask the right questions. In addition, the adviser you choose should not hint that the law can be evaded or suggest that he or she has found a foolproof scheme that cleverly takes advantage of the opportunities for tax savings available by law. Heed the warning that the IRS delivers every year: Beware the tax preparer who promises to get you a larger tax refund than another qualified preparer.

Above all, remember the moral of the old Burns and Allen routine in which Gracie rushes out and buys a lot of expensive objects on sale. As she explains to George, she totaled the amount she saved on each item until it was enough to pay for her purchases. It's funny onstage; it can be a horror in real life.

Do you think anybody would believe that tax savings can be achieved without actually spending the money to earn them? Read on.

1

IRAs AND KEOGH PLANS

NEWS FLASH: TAX EXPERTS AGREE!

Put simply, every working American should establish an IRA (and, for self-employed individuals, a Keogh plan—see page 18). That is the opinion of almost every tax expert, financial planning counselor, or investment adviser. The IRA, known in the trade as Everyman's tax shelter, is considered a fundamental tax-saving instrument, whether you make so many millions that it might seem a negligible consideration or make less than the maximum you can invest annually.

The IRA and Keogh have an assortment of advantages offered by no other tax-saving scheme: they're simple, can be very conservative and reliable (if you choose), have flexibility, are widely encouraged by the financial community (institutions will be competing for your business—always an advantage for the consumer), and can be initiated with a surprisingly low investment. In fact, financial experts generally express astonishment that at least 65 percent of those eligible to open an IRA have not yet done so (and are probably complaining that they can't find adequate tax relief).

The law currently allows you as an individual worker to set aside up to $2,000 of your income each year in an IRA. A couple can invest up to $2,250 when only one spouse is employed or $4,000 when both are working. In each case, of course, the amount put into an IRA is subtracted from the taxpayer's individual taxable income or, if the couple chooses to file jointly, joint taxable income. Until the funds are withdrawn no tax is imposed on the accumulated interest income or other appreciation in value, provided you do not borrow from your IRA or pledge it as security for a loan.

How much do you save in any one year? Multiply the amount invested in the IRA by the percentage of your tax bracket. A working couple in the 42 percent tax bracket—not at all a stratospheric percentile, thanks to inflation, an expanding economy, and other social factors—might decide to invest the limit ($4,000) in their IRA. Multiplied by 42 percent, this amount will yield the couple a tax savings for the year of $1,680.

In one sense, this couple has "spent," or invested, $4,000 to save $1,680 in taxes. The original amount, however, is not lost; it will grow in value, unless they choose extremely unsound investment strategies, and can be retrieved in the future. The reasoning is that the couple can afford to set aside the money until age 59½ or later, when their joint income may have dropped and will therefore be taxed at a lower rate. The age requirements are important. If you take money out of an IRA before you are 59½, the amount will be taxed; in addition, 10 percent of the amount will be due the IRS as a penalty, unless you are disabled. After age 70½, you must start making IRA withdrawals geared to your life expectancy. A penalty may be imposed for insufficient distributions.

Simple as it is, then, setting up an IRA demands that you work within the stated restrictions: (1) the amount you or you and your spouse can put into the plan annually; and (2) the age, 59½, before which monies *cannot* be withdrawn without penalties and tax loss, and the age, 70½, by which monies *must* be withdrawn.

THE FUTURE: CAN YOU AFFORD IT?

The IRA may not sound as alluring as some tax-saving plans, unless you ponder a couple of pretty vital statistics. First of all, there's life itself. The average American born today is likely, according to the most informed estimates, to live to be 73 years old. What with the strains on Social Security, the likelihood of cycles of dramatically increased inflation over the next few decades, and the growing resistance of many companies to substantial retirement plans for employees, most people in their later years are going to need the economic cushioning of increased retirement monies. As our older relatives have always told us, the future always comes sooner than we think.

What might you have when the future does come? To make a conservative estimate, consider what happens if, at age 25, you initiate an IRA plan that yields only 5 percent annually. If you faithfully invest $2,000 each year of your working life, the total accumulation when you retire at age 65 will be $242,000, a sum that (as we have seen) can continue to grow until age 70½, when you must begin withdrawals. If you invest in a plan that yields 10 percent (and many are offered in today's investment climate), the amount available to you on the brink of retirement would be $885,000, a sum likely to be quite substantial even four decades from now, unless inflation wildly outruns the patterns of history.

This amount, of course, will be taxed as you draw upon it, but (most likely) at a lower rate.

RETIREMENT TOO GOLDEN: A PROBLEM OF THE FEW

A few, a *very* few, retirees may, thanks to a solid IRA in combination with other retirement programs, encounter one of those problems that's hard to sympathize with until you have it yourself: too much retirement income.

Don't veer away from an IRA because of this possibility, however, because it is indeed an outside chance. If you have contributed throughout your working life to a tax-sheltered savings plan made available by your employer, *and* if you have stayed with a company for forty years and earned full pension benefits, you *could* retire and find yourself in a tax bracket higher than when you worked. It is an eventuality you should discuss with your tax adviser.

For most people, however, the possibility of making more money and being taxed in a higher bracket after retirement is slim. Only about 25 percent of working Americans stay with an employer long enough to become eligible for a pension, and even fewer are participating in employer-sponsored tax-sheltered savings plans.

IRAs: SO GOOD THAT PETER WILL PAY PAUL

In fact, rather than worrying about the possible consequences of having too much money in an IRA, most working Americans should concentrate instead on starting an IRA account *right now,* even if they have to borrow to do so.

Why does this make sense? Because the interest you pay on a bank loan is tax-deductible, and the interest or other yield in your IRA account is accumulating perfectly tax-free. Consult your banker about the figures. In today's market, it is likely that after factoring the tax break you get, you will wind up earning more from your IRA than you are paying for the use of the bank's money.

There are other strategies that will help you start an IRA (and that will have the added benefit of getting you in the habit of annual investment and long-range tax-savings planning):

The Tax Refund That Never Saw Vegas

Rather than treat your tax refund as a windfall, an excuse to celebrate or take an extra vacation trip, plan to use it for repaying part of any loan you take out to fund your IRA. Take the IRA deduction on your income tax form and, if you choose to itemize deductions, include the interest on the loan. When your tax refund check arrives, swallow hard and apply it to your loan. We're not saying that you should never take an unexpected vacation (money's no fun when it's no fun), but we are stressing that one of the most important financial steps you can take is to get into the habit of investing in an IRA. Once it's initiated, you'll be surprised how much easier it will be to contribute each year. As with any journey, that first step is at once the most difficult—and the most critical.

The "Ghost" Deduction That's Perfectly Legal

Here's a concept that may startle you if you tend to be literal-minded about money matters. According to the IRS (an institution not generally known for flights of fancy), you can claim a deduction for your IRA on your tax form even if you have not made the contribution. The catch, of course, is that you must make the contribution by April 15 of the year following the year being taxed.

Here's how this system might work. You file your tax return for 1985 as early as possible, claiming an IRA deduction of $2,000. Depending upon the computers at your regional IRS service center, you might receive your tax refund check anywhere from four to eight weeks after you file, if you file early enough. You have until April 15, 1986, according to the law, to deposit that $2,000 in the IRA. Your refund check may furnish all or part of that amount. (If you've begun an IRA in the past, you should pay special attention to a change in the law: Previous to tax year 1985, you could contribute to your IRA until August 15 of the year following the year for which you were filing—in other words, until the deadline for extensions. This is no longer allowed. All contributions to an IRA have to be made by the April 15 tax-filing date.)

Fund an IRA with Extra Deductions

This is another method, also perfectly legal, to help you save for your IRA. It requires that you be disciplined, though, or you will come up short at the end of the year. Simply file a new W-4 form with your employer, adding two exemptions. The extra take-home pay resulting should be deposited in your IRA account.

You should probably take a stern look at your spending habits before trying this method. If you cannot discipline yourself to deposit the additional take-home pay, you might not have enough at the end of the tax year to fund an IRA, and you will therefore be liable to pay taxes on the amount produced by the additional exemptions. The point of any good tax-savings plan is to give you an increased sense of security; don't let this one drive you up the wall when tax bills are due. Another alternative is to make IRA deposits in installments throughout the year, using the extra take-home pay from additional exemptions. Most banks and other institutions allow you to make a small initial payment and then add to it. If you do this, your investment return will vary on each deposit according to the then prevailing rates.

FINE-TUNING: A FEW USEFUL HINTS

If you don't have a problem with ready cash, you would be wise to put money in your account on January 2 or as soon thereafter as possible. The difference in earning power between deposits made early in the year and later can be dramatic. One financial analyst has calculated that a pattern of early contributions can add tens of thousands of dollars to the typical IRA account over a period of twenty to thirty years.

There are also sound psychological reasons for making an IRA contribution. If you have the money early in the year, you can avoid the temptation to spend it impulsively by investing it. Once it's invested, you can regard the amount as "spent" and concentrate on making more. Remember that the best time to save money is when you have it.

Savings can be increased for a couple when one spouse does not work, if the working partner owns a business with a legitimate reason for employing his or her spouse part-time. If the compensation is reasonable and records are carefully kept to show that actual work has been performed, then the spouse's salary can be invested in an IRA up to $2,000, thus raising the couple's limit from $2,250 to $4,000. Typically, such part-time work is as receptionist or bookkeeper in a company, perhaps to substitute for vacationing or ill regular employees. Any form of part-time work is acceptable to the IRS, however, provided that it is not "makework."

Keep in mind that the IRA might have related tax-deductible expenses. The cost of this book or of any other informational item is deductible; other deductible costs might include expenses billed to you by the IRA trustee for maintaining your account. Rather than have these expenses deducted from your annual contribution, as is generally the case, ask that they be billed separately to you. On certain kinds of brokerage accounts or mutual funds, you might add up to $30 a year to your IRA plan, while taking a tax deduction in that amount under "Miscellaneous" (if you choose to itemize deductions on your income tax form). These may seem like petty matters, but to be aware of them is to establish a pattern of thinking about tax deductions in an organized fashion. Besides, $30 a year will mean quite a bit over the years as your tax-deferred earnings are compounded.

PAYOFF: AN UNEXPECTED DIVIDEND

After a certain period of time, an IRA or Keogh investor will reach a break-even point at which it might make financial sense to withdraw all or part of the IRA or Keogh funds, the 10 percent penalty and consequent taxes notwithstanding. At that break-even point, the investor could be better off than if he had invested the same amount in a non-sheltered account.

As a matter of fact, there are a great many financial consultants who recommend the IRA as a convenient, psychologically painless method of saving for predictable large expenses in (relatively speaking) the short term—a down payment for a house, for example, or your children's college education. Here again it pays to look at the figures as they relate to your particular situation and find out exactly when you will be better off than you would have been by saving and investing in an account without the shelter advantages of an IRA. To determine your break-even point, discuss your investment with a qualified tax consultant.

Take the example of a couple who want to initiate an IRA to prepare for the projected increasing costs of a college education. If they are in the 35 percent tax bracket and choose an IRA plan that will yield a 10 percent annual return, they will pass the break-even point after only 5½ years. During those years and, in fact, until the moment they decide to withdraw funds for their child's education, they will have had all the advantages of an IRA: tax-deferred interest or other profits, ease of investment, lower annual tax bills. Although an IRA is really most effective as an instrument for retirement saving, this secondary use can be very helpful—and financially efficient—in long-range planning. CAUTION: Don't go overboard and think of the IRA as a short-term safety net for emergency expenses. You're likely to be the loser in such situations.

A QUICK REFRESHER: THE HIGHLIGHTS

1. Basically a retirement plan, the IRA usually should not be touched until you reach age 59½, at least, and must be touched by age 70½.

2. The money contributed and the interest or other profits earned are not taxed until you withdraw funds.

3. An IRA should be a number-one tax-savings priority, even if you have to borrow money or use your tax refund to contribute to it.

4. The earlier in the year you contribute to your IRA, the more tax-deferred income you will receive.

SOUND INVESTMENTS: MUST THEY BE BORING?

So far, we haven't really discussed the kinds of investments you might want to make when you contribute to your IRA. Choosing an investment is, in part, a matter of personal preference; if you are conservative in money matters, you are likely to consider options that would be less exciting for the investor who likes a little adventure. Another factor, of course, is the state of the economy and its various elements; investments that are highly recommended now might look much less attractive in three months, and vice versa. And no matter what your individual temperament, there's the age factor to consider: as you near retirement, it is probably not the best idea to begin putting your IRA contributions in wildly speculative stocks.

In short, you have to look at your own feelings about money, the current state of the economy, and the number of years you have left before retirement. Are you the kind of person who does not naturally take to speculative investing? No matter how promising or glamorous, an investment scheme is not worth losing sleep over.

For this reason you cannot (frustrating as it is) expect a wise and honest tax counselor to name "the best" investment, unless you make the personal factors clear. There is no best investment for an

IRA or for any other tax-savings plan. The facts and figures may look impersonal on paper; but investments must be matched with the personality of the investor.

Let's look at a few options for your IRA.

An IRA in the Bank

Banks, savings and loans institutions, and credit unions are ready and eager to encourage you to set up an IRA. Plans differ, and you should always be on the lookout for possible monthly maintenance charges or other extraneous fees. Generally speaking, however, the competition of the marketplace continues to ensure that major banking institutions will offer a low-risk, moderate-yield investment plan. Most common is the Certificate of Deposit (known in trade jargon as the CD), which is insured by the federal government for up to $100,000. You may choose a plan with fixed rates or fluctuating rates (tied to general interest rates). By law, the bank must tell you how much money your CD will earn over the entire investment period up to your retirement, if the yield is fixed rate. With fixed-rate plans, however, time is important. A CD may extend for a few months or for a few years: the longer the CD term, the higher the fixed interest rate will be...and that's a definite clue. The financial community currently believes that interest rates will continue to hold steady or rise over the next few years. If you choose a long-term fixed-rate plan—if you "lock in" today's interest rates, as the phrase goes, you might lose money if the rates rise. On the other hand, if rates go down during the life of your fixed-rate CD, your IRA continues to earn interest at the higher figure. As you see, even in the relatively conservative world of bank CDs, you will have to make highly personal investment decisions. Fixed or floating interest rates? Only you can decide.

★ You might find that it will be difficult to open a moderate-yield IRA account below a minimum of $250 or so; start anyway, even with low interest rates, then transfer when you've been able to build up your investment.

Mutual Funds

You probably have to be over thirty to remember how glamorous mutual funds used to be; to some investors they still are. Many people have done very well with mutual funds, but there are disadvantages that somewhat offset the attractive features.

In short, a mutual fund pools investor money to build a diversified portfolio, presumably spreading the risk over a variety of stocks and bonds while freeing the individual investor from having to agonize over each individual stock and bond investment. Mutual funds are best suited to the investor who can live happily with a calculated risk—and they can produce substantial gains; after all, the country's economic history shows that in the long run no investment performs as well as stocks. But they are subject to the unpredictable and widely swinging forces of the market. For an IRA, you are best advised to avoid funds that specialize in highly speculative stocks or commodities and instead seek out mutuals that concentrate on money market funds, bonds offering high current income, and common stocks likely to appreciate over time. You will also want to stay away from tax-exempt mutuals; by definition, your IRA is already tax-exempt, and these funds tend to offer a somewhat lower yield on your investment.

Should you choose mutuals? Remember that they are risky; they are not insured; and fees may be involved. Nevertheless, as we stress again and again in this book, the final choice must be yours.

Hands-On Involvement: The Stock Market

Knowledgeable about the market and eager to try out your knowledge in action? If you really love the excitement, challenge, and suspense of the stock market, *and* if you've built up a sizable IRA over a period of several years, you might want to open a self-directed account at a brokerage firm. In this type of IRA, you choose which stocks to buy and sell, although your broker, as custodian of the account, will receive a commission on each of your trades.

Obviously a small account cannot be diversified and will incur comparatively high brokerage fees. With a fairly large investment, however, you can have the pleasure of building your retirement account based upon your own analyses of the market and the risks involved. Serious research and constant alertness to trends can pay off—if you are drawn to this type of activity, you might indeed have "the gift." On the other hand, you should not try to run your own IRA account unless you have educated yourself about the pros and cons—you have to *want* to play the market and keep on top of developments relevant to your account, or the yield won't be worth the human effort.

★ Shop around for a discount brokerage firm; you'll pay less in commissions for trades.

EVEN BETTER THAN AN IRA: THE KEOGH PLAN

A Keogh plan is an even better investment plan than an IRA, but only self-employed taxpayers are eligible for it. If you are self-employed or have some income that comes from "moonlighting," up to 20 percent of that income *or* $30,000, whichever is the smaller, can be put aside annually in a Keogh plan for your retirement. Like an IRA investment, the Keogh contribution is deductible from your taxable income for the year you make the contribution, and the account's interest or other profits are not subject to taxes until you begin to withdraw funds. (Another advantage to a Keogh is that upon withdrawal, lump-sum distribution may receive favorable tax treatment. If you qualify, the tax you pay on the withdrawal may be reduced under a ten-year averaging rule. IRAs do not qualify for this benefit.)

You can have both an IRA and a Keogh, as long as you are wholly or partially self-employed. You have the same investment options for the Keogh as for the IRA and the same restrictions and penalties for early withdrawal of funds. Consider your situation carefully before deciding that you aren't eligible for a Keogh; it is estimated that at least nine million taxpayers are.

A FINAL WORD

Dull, conventional, and stodgy—these are the words a high roller might apply to IRA and Keogh plans, but these tax-savings schemes make sense for the typical American taxpayer. Wisely managed, they will ease your current tax burden as they build up financial security for your future. You're not likely to corner the market, but IRAs and Keogh plans have proven to be the most efficient tax-saving devices and retirement enhancement instruments yet devised. They are recommended by virtually all experts in tax planning and personal-finance management, which makes them highly unusual indeed when compared with other strategies for reducing your income taxes.

2

TAX-FREE AND TAX-DEFERRED INVESTMENTS

It's possible that every age is defined by certain status symbols—items of conspicuous consumption that represent ambitions of the day, such as a swimming pool shaped like a kidney, a second car in the garage, or a vacation home in the mountains. Of the current aspirations you might hear a lot about "tax-free" investment or the "munis." One of the nation's best-known humorists frequently rails in his column against TV and radio ads that encourage us to "chisel" the government out of taxes; and his reaction underscores what many people seem to feel about municipal bonds—that they are a free ride designed primarily for the wealthy.

Not necessarily so—thanks to inflation, increased salaries, two-worker families, and what used to be called "bracket creep," tax-free municipals may make sense for you and your family. If you are in the 30 percent tax bracket, for example, a yield of 6 percent on a tax-exempt bond would work out to be the same as a yield of 8.5 percent on a taxable corporate bond. If you are in the 42 percent tax bracket, the same 6 percent tax-exempt yield would actually work out to be 10.3 percent. As a glance at the morning paper will show you, however, most municipal bonds today are offering more substantial yields than a mere 6 percent. Also, more and more Americans, single people and couples, are finding themselves in or precipitously near the 50 percent bracket. At that level, the 10 percent yield on a tax-free municipal would be the equivalent of a 20 percent yield from a taxable investment. Such returns only become meaningful, of course, if you have a significant amount to invest or intend to build up a large investment over the years. Munis won't be right for you unless you are willing to tie up significant sums of money for a fairly long time...*and* will be satisfied with returns that are, even if tax-exempt, accurately described as conservative (compared to more flexible, risky financial instruments). On the other hand, you may not have all that much time to make up your mind; some analysts predict that the supply of new tax-exempt municipals will shrink in the near future because of surpluses in many municipalities.

TAX-EXEMPT *AND* WORRY-FREE: WHAT'S THE CATCH?

No investment is entirely worry-free, but in the minds of most fledgling investors, municipal bonds come pretty close. You can't get in for less than $5,000; that is, if you want to invest in a new municipal issue. It is possible, however, to find a "unit trust," or fixed portfolio of municipal bonds, with an investment minimum as low as $1,000. If you have more than that to invest, munis can act as a conservative balancing factor in your portfolio. Some people find it easier to take risks elsewhere when they have a sizable investment in municipals.

State Taxes May Apply

Be warned that municipal bonds, which are issued to fund development projects by the governments of cities, counties, and states and by certain special agencies, are *federally* tax-exempt to all taxpayers, but *state taxes* apply if you are not a resident of the state of issue. It is sensible, therefore, to purchase munis issued in your own state, especially if you happen to live in such high income-tax states as New York, Connecticut, Massachusetts, or New Jersey. An exception to this is Puerto Rico, which is considered to be a part of the federal government; consequently, your state will not levy taxes on bonds issued in Puerto Rico.

★ Bonds issued by your local municipality are also free from local taxes.

SCHOOLS, SEWERS, STREETS: HOW TO CHOOSE

Since you will be purchasing your municipals from your broker, you are likely to hear that there is diversity even in the municipals market. Not all bonds offer the same tax-exempt yields; there are different bond ratings and different degrees of security and guarantee.

Just When You Thought It Was Safe to Go Back In

Yes, you will keep hearing that munis are a safe investment, but there are degrees of safety. In fact, although it is a very rare event, it sometimes happens that a municipal bond is forced to default. You should, therefore, choose only those munis that are rated A or better by Moody's or Standard & Poor's.

★ Few A-rated bonds have ever defaulted on a debt. Some bonds rate as high as AAA or as low as C on Moody's scale, or D for "default" in the S&P ratings.

If you write away for information about municipals and your name gets on the mailing or phone list of an aggressive brokerage firm, you may find yourself bombarded with information about low-rated, high-yield bonds (often called "junk" by insiders). Financial advisers generally agree that you should avoid such adventures, at least until you have established a more conservative portfolio in municipals. You can't expect a muni to offer contradictory attractions, both safety *and* unusually high yields. Municipals are for the average investor seeking reliable, tax-exempt income; they are not for gambling. You'll be doing well enough, thank you, with today's high yields and your own rising tax bracket. Stick to the A's, at least in the beginning.

In addition, you should probably choose bonds that carry a guarantee from the federal government or have been insured to term. Insured bonds will probably have slightly lower yields than uninsured issues, but the increase in safety may be worth the slight cost in terms of reduced tax-exempt income. Should the bond issuer default, insurance guarantees you payment of interest plus principal.

Should you try to "lock in" the yields? Many financial consultants think so (obviously some bond specialists tend to be a bit more conservative in their advice than experts attracted to other types of investment). If you want to guarantee the rates being offered currently, have your broker select munis that cannot be redeemed early by issuers (or "called," as the trade would have it) for at least 10 years.

★ A good broker has your best interest at heart; he also has to eat regularly. Be sure to make abundantly clear your distaste for paying hefty commissions for nickel-and-dime actions. In other words, find out ahead of time what the charges are going to be for the different kinds of purchases you are considering. If your objective is to invest in several different municipalities, the best way for you to avoid multiple commissions may be to invest in a municipal bond fund—see page 25.

THE LIQUIDITY FACTOR

With careful planning, an investor can sometimes have it both ways: the long-term guarantee of a high tax-exempt yield from a municipal coupled with the ability to sell the bond quickly whenever you decide. You can sell your bond, of course, only when someone is willing to buy. For best liquidity, then, you should only select bonds issued by well-known and highly regarded entities. As economic and political conditions rise and fall, some municipalities will for a period of time have a "better press than others... and vice versa. Public perception affects the market potential of tax-exempt municipals, as it does any other commodity. If liquidity is a principal concern for you, buy munis that have (and are likely to continue to have) a "good rep" because the issuing municipality, state government, or agency has a good track record in the public eye.

BOND FUNDS: SAFETY IN NUMBERS

Previously mentioned as a way of reducing the commissions on your munis, bond mutual funds also have the advantage of liquidity. Whenever you choose, the fund will buy back all or part of your investment at the current market price, be it more or less than the amount you originally paid. In addition, bond mutual funds lessen the risks of your investment, since the professional managers of the fund will select a large and diversified portfolio, balancing conservative purchases against, perhaps, the occasional low-rated but potentially promising "muni." Of course, along with the advantages of liquidity, lowered commissions, and increased safety, you still receive the benefits of yields that are completely tax-exempt.

Diversification, at Least Cost

For the beginning investor and the relatively small muni investment (say, from the usual fund minimum of $1,000 to $5,000 or so), the managed bond mutual fund should be considered. In today's market, fund managers are competing for your business, and that is all to your advantage. Above all, you will discover that successful managers will make investing convenient; some funds even offer such side advantages as the ability to write checks against the value of your shares. Usually, the tax-exempt interest earned by your investment will be automatically reinvested in your account, unless you decide otherwise.

★ Funds will be termed either "load" or "no-load" —the former having a sales charge because they are offered through brokers, the latter free of such charges because they are sold directly by management. To date, performances of the two types of bond funds appear to be similar; therefore, it seems best to avoid unnecessary sales charges, which can total as much as 8 percent of your initial investment, and stick with a no-load fund.

Fixed Yields, for Less than $25,000

The type of bond fund known as a unit trust may be attractive if you are investing less than $25,000 and are especially interested in locking in a fixed tax-exempt yield. The unit trust requires a $1,000 minimum investment and a one-time brokerage fee of approximately 3 to 4 percent of your investment in the fund.

As with the bond mutual fund, a professional manager has chosen a widely diversified portfolio in order to lessen risk, perhaps spreading the investment of the fund among as many as twenty or thirty bond issues that meet the fund's standards for rate or yield and safety of investment. But there is a crucial difference between the unit trust and the managed bond mutual fund: as the difference in terminology might suggest, the former is essentially unmanaged, a "closed-end trust" with the bonds in the fund selected and prepackaged up front. New issues are not added; as the individual bonds reach maturity, the unit trust is gradually liquidated.

Affordable and fairly secure, the unit trust is not wholly without risk, because bond prices (and therefore unit trust prices) will fluctuate in response to the movement of interest rates (prices will fall as general interest rates begin to rise and vice versa). In the meantime, the monthly income from your investment is a fixed, tax-free amount. The expectation is that when your unit investment trust reaches full maturity (which might be at ten, twenty, thirty years or more after you invest), you will get back the amount you originally invested. If you decide to sell in the interim, however, the vagaries of the market will determine whether you can sell at a price lower or higher than you originally paid.

★ The most highly recommended unit trust is known as a "single state trust." The bonds in the trust are tax-exempt at all three levels of government taxing activity—federal, state, and local—and tend to be of good quality, issued within a single state but covering a variety of public programs.

TAX-EXEMPT ZERO BONDS

If you really dislike the uncertainty of a tax-exempt investment, there is a way to determine exactly how much money you need to invest today in order to get a specified return on your investment at a specified date in the future.

The "zero coupon bond" is so called because the investor is paid no interest during the term of the bond but receives it all at maturity. Meanwhile, a $1,000 bond, which is sold at a discount well below the ordinary market price, increases in value at a compound rate. It has recently been possible, for example, to put down less than $100 for a bond that will mature in twenty years at $1,000 or to invest between $250 and $300 in a bond that will mature at $1,000 in ten years. (Rates vary, of course, and are subject to market fluctuations; it pays to shop around.)

Tax-exempt zero bonds have a unique feature that distinguishes them from other zeros. The IRS collects taxes annually on the interest gained by a taxable zero coupon bond, even though that interest will not be paid over until the maturity of the bond. This would be true, for example, in the case of corporate zero bonds or zero coupon bonds offered by the U.S. Treasury. On tax-exempt zero bonds, however, the interest is not subject to taxes at the federal level. Tax-exempt zero bonds are offered by municipalities, states, and certain agencies; like municipal bonds, they are not taxed by the cities or states in which they are issued for sale.

★ Tax-exempt zero bonds do not pay as high a rate as the many different types of taxable zero coupon bonds.

Aside from earning tax-exempt interest, the tax-exempt zero coupon bond can provide psychological security as well, because you know precisely how much you will receive on the date of maturity. Financial advisers cite the zero as a relatively painless and worry-free investment for parents who will in years to come need to finance their children's education or for the mortgage holder who faces a sizable balloon payment on his mortgage sometime in the future.

If you want to fine-tune the advantages of this financial instrument with an eye to possible inflationary pressures and the accompanying increase in interest rates, consider buying tax-exempt zero coupon bonds with relatively short periods of maturity. Conceivably, inflation would cause a drop in the price of the zero; if your first zero were to mature at that point, you could then buy the less expensive zero.

★ Frustrating as it may be to the investor who doesn't want to worry about his or her investments, no one can tell with certainty whether or not to expect a sharp rise in inflation in the near future. Whether or not to choose your investments by predicting the course of inflation is up to you; it's a personal decision. Would it be as much fun otherwise?

U.S. GOVERNMENT SECURITIES

Small Change Adds Up

U.S. savings bonds may not sound as glamorous as other investment opportunities, but they offer tax advantages for the beginning investor who is patiently planning for the future. Series EE bonds, with interest exempt from state and local taxes, can pay from 7.5 percent annually to as much as 11.5 percent (or more, depending upon a formula tied to the average yields of five-year treasury securities). To receive the minimum guaranteed 7.5 percent, the bonds must be held at least five years. New bonds have a ten-year term, but the Treasury typically allows extensions.

Owners of EE bonds may elect to defer tax on the bonds until maturity, instead of having the interest taxed annually. If deferral is elected, tax must be paid on the accumulated interest upon final maturity of the bonds (after extensions), unless they are rolled over to series HH bonds.

HH's have a ten-year maturity and are available in denominations ranging from $500 to $10,000. Just exchange your mature series EE bonds for series HH bonds, thereby postponing your tax bill. The IRS does require that taxes be paid annually on the series HH bonds, however, even as you gain the use of the tax-deferred dollars from your original series EE investment.

Safe and Competitive

"Supersafe," as they've been called in the investment trade, U.S. Treasury bonds, notes, or bills are generally considered an essential for the thoughtful investor. Added to safety (the government's guarantee to pay the principal back to you at maturity) are significant tax advantages, if you live in a community where taxes are high; interest earned on all these treasury securities is exempt from state and local taxes. The amount saved, of course, will depend upon your local tax obligations.

In addition, the yields on Treasury bonds, notes, and bills tend to be competitive these days, because the record U.S. deficit is covered by these three investment vehicles and the government is borrowing money at high interest rates, just as other borrowers must. The money supply, too, is relatively "tight" (as of this writing)—another factor that ups the yields on treasuries.

★ Another attractive feature of U.S. Government securities is that, in contrast with most municipals, all Treasury notes and most Treasury bonds cannot be redeemed by the issuer before maturity. In investment jargon, they cannot be "called" or do not "have a call feature," which would force you, the investor, to give up the bonds for cash on a specific date set by the government.

The differences between the three types of U.S. securities have to do with length of maturity, minimum investment, and type of payment. For T-bills, the minimum investment is $10,000; the maturities are short-term: thirteen, twenty-six and fifty-two weeks. They sell below face value rather than pay interest. The maturities for treasury notes range from one to ten years. Notes due in less than four years require a minimum investment of $5,000; longer-term notes are available for a minimum investment of $1,000. For treasury bonds, the minimum investment is also $1,000; maturities range from ten to thirty years.

If you have a diversified portfolio, it may be convenient simply to purchase U.S. securities through your broker, but by buying directly from the government you might save from $25 to $75 on commissions. Just contact the regional office of the Treasury Department nearest you or a nearby Federal Reserve Bank; either will send you the request order forms for T-bills. You can also write the Bureau of Public Debt, Dept. N., Washington, D.C. 20239.

There are mutual funds that invest primarily in U.S. securities, but the dividends on your shares in such funds might be subject to state and local taxes.

Safe, with good yields and tax advantages, U.S. securities also offer that inestimable quality of maximum liquidity. Interest accrues daily during the term of your security, so you can sell without loss at any time before maturity.

★ It may be worth the effort to contact discount brokers when you decide to sell; those who are willing to buy treasury notes, bonds, and bills will charge a lower sales commission than a full-service broker.

TAX-DEFERRED ANNUITIES AND LIFE INSURANCE

Chances are, if you discuss your financial situation with a tax planner, you will hear warm praise for such insurance industry products as tax-deferred annuities and life insurance policies that combine insurance protection with tax-deferred income. Reason: A high percentage of professional tax planners are also licensed insurance agents, reaping commissions on sales and subsequent renewal of insurance policies and annuities. Nevertheless, tax-deferred returns are enticing in and of themselves, and the cautious investor might find them worthwhile, albeit not quite so beneficial as his or her planner believes.

Because of a couple of large and well-publicized bankruptcies last year involving insurance companies that had specialized in sales of tax-deferred annuities, the financial community has decided to move very circumspectly in this field. First of all, it is recommended that you buy tax-deferred annuities only from an insuror that is rated no less than A by Best's Insurance Reports. In addition, you should use your common sense; when an annuity is being offered at 3 to 4 percent above prevailing market rates, it is probably wise to decline. Only a remarkably strong company portfolio could pay you the unusually high rate and at the same time turn a profit. This is an extremely unlikely combination; why, you must ask yourself, has such a fine deal not been snapped up by other investors? Also, consider dealing only with insurance companies that are (along with their parent companies) licensed for operation in either California or New York, states recognized for stringent enforcement of regulations.

A LONG-TERM INVESTMENT

What exactly are you buying? The tax-deferred annuity is a savings plan offered by an insurance company and can be one of two types: fixed or variable. The latter can be considered a kind of mutual fund, with a choice of investments ranging from stocks to bonds to securities in the money market; consequently, your return on the annuity will fluctuate with the constituent investments. The fixed annuity, on the other hand, is comparable to a CD: the principal and a designated rate of return are guaranteed for a term of from a few months up to five years. With this type of tax-deferred annuity, you would do well to select a plan that has a so-called bailout clause, which allows you to withdraw your investment penalty-free should the return rate fall a percentage point or two below what it was initially. Then you can transfer your investment to an annuity paying higher rates.

Remember that you are buying the tax-deferred annuity with your taxable income (unless, of course, it is part of your IRA or Keogh plan). Taxes on your earnings are deferred until you withdraw your funds. Because the IRS demands a 5 percent penalty on most withdrawals made from your tax-deferred annuity before age 59½, this type of investment is most suitable for long-term savings. (The 5 percent penalty on withdrawals made before age 59½ applies only to the extent the cash value exceeds the investment in the contract. It does not apply at all if you are disabled, or if the withdrawal is part of an annuity for life or a period of at least five years.)

★ Another new trick for the old dogs already familiar with tax-deferred annuities: On contracts issued before January 16, 1985, the 5 percent penalty applies only to taxable withdrawals made from investments held for less than ten years.

For contracts issued after January 15, 1985, all taxable withdrawals are subject to the penalty; the ten-year exception does not apply.

THE COMBINATION: INSURANCE PLUS TAX-DEFERRED INCOME

If you have the patience, shop around for a low-cost life insurance policy that offers both tax-deferred income and insurance protection; you may be pleased with the features provided by such plans. A universal life policy gives insurance along with investment in a money market savings account; a variable life policy offers insurance along with investment in mutual funds.

Beware the sales fees and possible withdrawal penalties demanded by the insuror! Make sure you have a good reason for buying one of these policies rather than taking on a less expensive term policy and investing what you save in munis or tax-deferred annuities.

During the life of the universal or variable policy, you are not liable for taxes on the income; when you cash it in, however, you must pay taxes on everything except the premiums you've paid into the plan. By the way, the IRS does not impose a penalty for early withdrawal, in contrast with its penalty charges for early withdrawals from an IRA, Keogh plan, or tax-deferred annuity.

★ Income tax liability on the universal or variable life policy is not passed along to your beneficiary in the event of your death, just as it is not with any other form of life insurance.

) SUM UP...

e great risk of repeating a misconception is that the misconcep-n, not the correction, will be remembered. Nevertheless, it is obably a good idea at this point to remind the reader that all the ns discussed in this chapter require investment of funds from tax-le income. Only the interest or other profits that accrue to the vestments can be considered tax-free or tax-deferred.

To some this distinction may seem obvious, but tax counselors port that many first-time investors assume that a "tax-free invest-nent" is one in which the principal invested is not subject to tax. his is not so. Only funds invested in an IRA or Keogh plan are not xed—and even they (along with the monies they earn) will be xed at withdrawal time. The investments discussed in this chapter yield *tax-free income;* they do not carry tax waivers on the amount invested.

3

THE 1984 REVISIONS ON TAX SHELTERS

In this chapter we will begin a discussion of the tax shelter, a device that has captured the imagination of the media, of the morally casual and the greedy, of serious investors, and, perhaps most of all, of the average taxpayer who is curious about all the excitement and may feel rather peeved at being, presumably, left out of the action. First, however, a good introduction to this complicated, tantalizing, and constantly changing subject is in order. What exactly is a tax shelter? It's a limited partnership, involving an investment which may be in real estate, or oil or gas exploration, for example, designed to produce tax deductions for the limited partners.

Now let's take a look at the 1984 Tax Reform Act. This 770-page, 329-provision bill was in part a reaction to tax shelter abuses. In its effort to explain clearly what is not allowed, the legislation discloses the depth of misunderstanding and variety of chicanery that exists today in the world of sheltered income investments.

Unfortunately, the concept of the tax shelter has been widely misunderstood as a mechanism designed purely to yield losses as a tax write-off. Even more unfortunate, many highly creative promoters were able to put together shelter deals that gave some clients write-offs as high as five to one in the first year of the shelter investment—until the IRS stepped in and was not amused.

In fact, the shelter is an instrument of government policy designed to encourage investment in certain high-risk activities that the government feels are important to the economy or to national security (the drilling of new oil wells, for example) or to the well-being of society (such as housing for low-income families). Although observers might disagree about the relative merits of a specific program designated as a sheltered activity, it is clear that the laws have been written to benefit society, not the individual investor or even a class of investors. Consequently, to be legitimate, the shelter must actually involve some risk on the part of the investor and must also be designed with the expectation of making a profit.

These ideas will be discussed in more detail later, but let's look at some of the practices that were proscribed or altered by the 1984 tax changes.

THE 1984 CHANGES: A CURB ON FINAGLING

Registration Rules

To try to cope with the apparent flood of abusive tax shelters, the new legislation requires the investor to register with the IRS any tax shelter that is likely to provide more than a two-to-one tax write-off in any year over the first five years. This requirement was instituted to aid the agency's search for shelters that "utilize extreme, improper and even illegal interpretations of the law or involve incomplete or misleading facts in an attempt to secure for investors substantial tax benefits which are clearly disproportionate to the economic reality of the transactions." This is cold legal language, but one can almost sense the anger of the IRS lawyers. In simple terms, they are making clear that a tax shelter is not an excuse for fraud.

Changed Accounting Measures

Various types of shelters have allowed the investor to deduct business or interest expenses in the year *before* they are actually incurred. This is no longer allowed. The idea was to assist the taxpayer facing a large tax bill by permitting him to get a write-off as quickly as possible after his investment in the shelter. Typically, this transaction would take place in the last months of the year, and the actual expenses thus deducted on the income tax form would be paid off the following year or even later. According to analysts, the provision principally affected shelters in research and development ventures, cattle-feeding programs, and private real estate partnerships. Before the enactment of the 1984 provisions, investors in these kinds of shelters were promised a total tax write-off as high as four times the amount invested! A return this high is abusive and represents the kind of blatant misuse of the concept that has caused the government to scrutinize all shelters more intently and has also, it is safe to say, provoked a good deal of taxpayer cynicism about the intent and use of the shelter concept.

Stretched Depreciation Write-Offs

The new law has lengthened the depreciation on real estate from fifteen to eighteen years, thereby slightly lowering the annual tax write-offs on such investments. (An exception is property built as or converted to low-income housing, which still has a fifteen-year depreciation period.) Some analysts felt that syndicators were paying premium prices for real estate to take advantage of the fifteen-year term; it is their view that the longer depreciation period may well have the effect of bringing about a stabilization of real estate prices. The IRS was concerned that the shorter period was "overly generous" and "had contributed to the rapid growth of real estate partnerships that combined tax benefits in order to achieve low or even negative effective tax rates...in effect...a subsidy to such investments at the expense of more productive investments that had a higher pre-tax rate of return." In short, the public interest was being short-changed; some taxpayers were using shelters simply to avoid taxes.

Quarterly Estimated Payments of AMT (Alternative Minimum Tax)

First enacted in 1982, this tax was designed to ensure that wealthy taxpayers could not avoid paying a so-called fair share of taxes, or at least 20 percent of income, by using shelters to the hilt. In any year when a taxpayer's AMT is greater than his or her liability as computed with the use of shelters and other tax-saving schemes, the taxpayer is liable for the AMT. Starting in 1985, the AMT must be paid in quarterly estimated payments. The AMT can also be triggered when you take a large capital gain, but the principal thrust of the law is to reduce the abuses of tax shelters and tax advantages.

ARE SHELTERS STILL USEFUL?

As the foregoing suggests, the government is making a strenuous, concentrated effort to seek out and punish tax frauds disguised as legitimate tax shelters. Part of the effort involves stricter controls on procedures; part involves the imposition of sterner penalties for abuse (beginning January 1985, for example, interest on underpayment in tax shelter transactions will be 120 percent of the annual rate normally imposed on tax payment deficiencies—say, 13.2 percent when the normal annual interest rate is 11 percent). The government is also stressing that tax losses must be tied to actual risk and more closely related to actual expenses in the year when losses are claimed.

What we may have here is a communication failure, so before going into a description of some typical shelter activity, it would be a good idea to try to clear up the confusion. The rules have to be understood; the attitude of the government has to be understood; above all, the weary taxpayer must resist those ter ng legitimate "scams." When a tax shelter looks as soft and fleecy as a dozing canary and you feel a warm little grin curling your lips, it's more than likely you've discovered a shelter that will incur the wrath of the IRS. Shelters are not gold mines; they're devices that take work and care.

THE SHELTER: JUST WHAT IS IT?

So far we've noted some tax changes that underscore what a tax shelter is not and have indicated that many shelters (and the people who use them) are on the far side of the law—unabashedly so. Why such a less than enthusiastic introduction to the whole subject?

Answer: Tax shelters are complicated, complex, and bewildering tax and investment strategies that should be approached with caution and employed honestly, with a probity that Caesar's wife would envy.

Remember, the intent of a shelter is to give the investor a tax break in the short term, either in the form of deductions or tax credits, to encourage certain kinds of investments; in the long term, the IRS expects to recover some of the tax revenue it has forgone. A tax shelter is not supposed to enrich the investor at the expense of the tax-paying public.

The right approach has been defined by Robert Low, a Washington, D.C., accountant who is active in the area of tax shelters: "Be very cautious. This key element is easy to deal with conceptually, but hard to put into practice. Everyone should remember that a tax shelter is an investment and, as with any other type of investment, the only point is to produce a stream of cash. If the first criterion is to produce a tax loss, stay away from it. A tax shelter must have sound economic underpinning and the expectation that it will produce a cash profit."

There are many different kinds of tax shelters. All are designed to make a profit, furnish money to meet the venture's financial needs, and at the same time give tax benefits to the investors. In certain cases, and to an increasingly limited extent, the investor can increase his or her tax benefits by the use of what is called "leverage." That is, it is sometimes possible to pay for the deductible items of a shelter with borrowed money—in effect gaining tax deductions with the bank's money as well as your own.

The famous tax loss of a shelter results because for the first few years of the business venture the income will be significantly less than the investor's tax benefits. The tax loss is desirable for an investor who has large amounts of taxable income from other sources, because it can reduce his or her tax bill for the year (tax losses are only useful, therefore, to someone who has a large tax obligation for the year or years during which the shelter is producing tax benefits). In some shelter deals, all or most of the excess deductions occur in the first year of operation; in others (such as real estate) they are spread out over a period of several years. Remember, though, that these losses do not represent a permanent escape from the demands of the IRS. Like most of the tax-oriented forms of investment we have already discussed, tax shelters simply offer a deferral of taxes until a more propitious time for the investor: retirement, for example, or a year when the tax liability can be handled with relatively little financial discomfort. Make sure you understand this critical aspect of the tax shelter concept: taxes are deferred, not wiped out. In this light, read the following explanation of "cash flow" or "cash distribution."

The cash generated by a successful business venture is returned to the investors in a shelter as "cash flow" or "cash distribution." Distributions remain constant over the life of the deal, but tax benefits diminish after the first year or first few years. Gradually the shelter's deductible expenses decrease; the investor's taxable income increases, in effect, as the venture's tax benefits diminish.

The details of drawing up a venture that will maximize tax benefits to the investor without exposing him or her to large tax obligations in the future can be extremely complex. You cannot evaluate the adequacy and legitimacy of a shelter just by reading a short introduction to the subject. Although it is helpful to you to learn about the basics of the tax shelter concept, when it comes time to make the decisions about investment you need professional help: a lawyer who is knowledgeable about changes in the law, a tax accountant who is experienced in tax shelter deals. And mark those words "knowledgeable" and "experienced." Even before the 1984 changes in the law there was confusion about exactly what types of deals would work (not to mention what ventures would be sanctioned by the ever-watchful IRS). Today the situation is even more bewildering, and it seems likely that in future the laws applying to shelter deals will become stricter and will be more stringently enforced. Members of the government have ears, too; like many taxpayers, they have heard all about the exciting "killings" to be made in tax shelter activity. Efforts are afoot to bring a little more sobriety to the proceedings...and the investor, therefore, should strike a similarly sober note.

LOOK BEFORE YOU LEAP: WHAT (AND WHOM) TO AVOID

Scour the Past

Find out everything you can about the people who are promoting or managing the tax shelter that interests you. Anyone in this business should be willing to furnish you with relevant information such as audited reports of past deals and any possible conflicts of interest between the project you might join and other ventures the promoter is fostering. Is the manager financially secure or too harried with his own financial problems to give your project the attention it needs? How do his or her bank and credit references look? Does the promoter try to dodge your questions? Is there too much toothy optimism in the air?

Hold Back, Anyway

Even a manager or promoter with a sterling track record can put together a tax deal that might, to use self-explanatory jargon, "go belly-up." Even experienced, honest, cautious investors can have some plain bad luck. Of course, the experienced, honest, cautious promoter will remind you of this, but you may be too dazzled by his or her past successes to listen all that closely to reason. The word "risk" is not to be taken lightly—and don't set yourself up for the possibility of losses greater than you can afford. Look at the intangible and unpredictable factors in any shelter; many are completely out of the control of the individual manager or promoter.

Do You Need Eight Hours a Night?

The tax shelter investor almost always plays a passive role. You will most likely be engaged in a private partnership or public holding that will be managed on a day-to-day basis by professionals. You will be dependent upon the decisions of others, forced to rely upon their integrity and skill. To some investors, this situation is well-nigh anxiety-producing, if not intolerable. Add to this the unpredictable nature of such ventures as the drilling of oil wells, and you may well decide that the wear and tear on your nerves is not worth the possible tax benefits to be gained from the shelter. This is a matter to be discussed with your tax adviser. Unless you thrive on the challenge of the highly speculative shelter, you should probably avoid them; you may even find that all shelters are, by definition, too unpredictable and otherwise worrisome for your own tastes.

Know Your Investment

Even though you are a passive investor, you should choose ventures involving activities that are familiar or interesting to you. No matter how carefully you and your tax adviser study the prospectus of a shelter deal, you are really just looking at a promoter's projections. What about a real estate shelter that involves rehabilitation of the once fashionable downtown shopping street in your hometown? Or a housing project for low-income families that will bring new life to the area? If you care about the business venture, you are more likely to be able to judge the worth and intent of a shelter built around that venture. Some advisers counsel against shelters that include properties widely scattered over the country, since management resources may consequently be spread too thin. Other advisers warn that a shelter deal concentrated in one area may be too exposed to the possibility of a sudden local economic downturn. These considerations can be more sensibly evaluated when you know the business or other activity involved. Also, it's a good general rule that the best investment, tax shelter or not, is one you care about.

Not Too Weak, Not Too Strong

Once you understand that the bottom line of a shelter is not tax avoidance but tax deferral plus long-term profits, you will realize that the business venture must be adequately capitalized. With your lawyer or accountant, determine whether or not the promoters of your shelter have prepared for the unseen contingencies that could be reasonably associated with the particular venture, such as explosions at a new oil drilling site or long periods of foul weather at a construction site. Overfinancing is equally dangerous. Default and foreclosure are real possibilities when the interest payments of a leveraging loan are much too high to be supported by the income from the business venture. Even if a venture has been initiated with a "nonrecourse" loan (a concept to be discussed in the following chapter), the investor may incur a tax liability.

Prepare for Burnout

After four to seven years, certain tax shelter deals—such as equipment leasing and real estate—experience the phenomenon known appropriately as "burnout." Tax experts report that many investors, though warned of this eventuality, do not adequately prepare for its serious consequences (and will often blame their advisers for not warning them strongly enough). Burnout refers to the exhaustion of tax write-offs on a deal. Tax write-offs end, but the profits on the deal are still only paper (or "phantom") profits; consequently, the investor is not making enough real cash to cover his or her tax obligations. To prepare for burnout, you should have invested the tax savings of the first years of the shelter so that there will be money to cover the taxes that materialize later. Work out a plan with your accountant so that your tax benefits do not turn into a tax nightmare.

Don't Risk "No-Risk"

Occasionally a promoter will entice an investor by promising that income for a specific venture is certain to pay off the promissory note used to finance the undertaking or that the note will not have to be called; in other words, the investor is being told that he is not "at risk" for the money. In such a case, the IRS will not allow interest deductions on the note. Similarly, the agency may question and eventually disallow deductions taken by an investor for "ordinary and necessary" expenses. Have management fees been inflated so that investors can take larger deductions on their income tax statements? Beware any representations by promoters and managers of large tax benefits to be gained by manipulation of the intent of the law. You must be at risk, and the deductions on expenses must not be out of line. Always remember that the legitimacy of a shelter is the sum of its parts; each feature of the shelter must meet the standards of the government's "economic performance rule." Deductions are meant for expenses required to make an investment profitable. The IRS knows that you know what that means.

When a "Killing" Is Suicide

The most enthusiastically pursued IRS crackdown activity on tax shelters is the auditing of overpriced ventures. In effect, overpricing constitutes collusion between the promoters and the investors, no matter how inventive the latter may be in protesting their innocence. Promoters of overvalued shelters will reap huge profits; investors will receive inflated deductions. Much press has been devoted in recent months to overpricing in the art market and in the record industry, but the practice is not limited to exotic ventures. Don't feel that your shelter is safe because "everyone is doing it"; the significant number of overvalued shelters has impelled the government to expand its investigations. If an audit reveals that you have taken deductions based upon overvalued assets, your tax savings will be rolled back dramatically. In addition to the back taxes, of course, you will be liable for interest and penalty fees.

EVEN AS WE SPEAK...

Tax shelter law is constantly changing. Since 1976, there have been five legislative actions that have significantly affected the field; there will be more in the immediate future, according to the most informed guesses.

Why so much, so frequent revision? Part of the answer lies in the ingenuity of promoters, who find loopholes not intended by the government; these are then plugged and proscribed. Part of the answer lies in the complexity of the nation's financial structures, the diversity of its many different kinds of business enterprises, the competition for capital investment, the unique situation of the individual taxpayer, and the deep and reverberating mysteries of accounting.

★ Part of the answer, too, lies in the government's responsibility to its citizens. The law is written with the intent of protecting the citizenry as a whole from the unfair depredations of the few; it is also, however, written to protect the investor from unscrupulous promoters.

In any event, it is important to seek expert advice, particularly from professionals who are sensibly humble. One prominent New York accountant, for example, has admitted that he "simply cannot understand" certain aspects of the Tax Reform Act of 1984. At seminars of those in the field, he says, there is general agreement on the confused—and confusing—nature of one or more of the bill's provisions. In fact, the ink was scarcely dry on the legislation before Congress was already acting to clarify it...and they still are! So avoid the temptation to chase after the shelter that has been described by friends at lunch as a "steal" or "foolproof." What was considered an exciting and legitimate venture a few months ago may not be so now. Before making any kind of commitment, talk to your tax adviser.

These changes may also affect an investor already involved in a particular tax shelter—especially later on, when it comes time to sell out. Bewildering changes in tax law might discourage other investors from buying you out. Investor anxieties have a way of communicating themselves to others, and the current atmosphere of confusion doesn't help. To protect your long-term interests, exercise caution and financial adroitness.

To repeat: It is important to be aware of the latest amendments, revisions, and other changes in tax law. Find tax advisers who do their homework.

4
CHOOSING A SHELTER

"Losses are valuable things. Sell them to yourself before they are captured by someone less worthy. Everyone is trying to buy losses... it's the sizzle, not the steak."

—A lawyer in *Something to be Desired,* by Thomas McGuane

With due respect to the above amusing quote, there will be *no* sizzle in your tax shelter without the steak; you will be looking for a shelter that makes money as well as offers tax losses. Usually, the form your investment takes will be a "limited partnership" (sometimes called a "syndicate").

This ownership vehicle includes a general partner who manages the business venture. Ideally, of course, the general partner should be an investor in the shelter; the other investors are the limited partners. In most shelters, the liability of the investors is limited to the amount they have invested. Profit, loss, and tax benefits are allocated to partners on a predetermined sharing arrangement. "Under the federal income tax law, a partnership is not a taxable entity. Rather, the partnership taxable income or loss is determined at the partnership level and then passed through to the partners, who report such income or loss on their income tax returns."

In practice, the general partner is the promoter of the tax shelter. By law, he or she alone participates in the operation of the business. Naturally, as an investor you would expect this person to have some experience in both shelter activity and the business in which your shelter is being organized. After all, the very nature of a limited partnership carries some built-in disadvantages. For one thing, it is very difficult, time-consuming, and expensive for disillusioned limited partners to band together and sue for the removal of an incompetent, negligent, or fraudulent general partner. Even if successful, the limited partners might encounter a kind of double jeopardy: if they are correct in calling the general partner fraudulent in his dealings, it is possible that the deal itself will be termed a fraud by the IRS; the limited partners would lose the tax benefits already claimed in the transaction. For another thing, a limited partnership is not very liquid: it is considered too risky by banks to be used as collateral for a loan, should you suddenly find yourself in need of cash. More than likely you won't even be able to sell your investment to the general partner, although some limited partnerships allow for that possibility at a specified date. In general, you will be committed to the limited partnership for the term outlined in your partnership agreement or in the prospectus describing the partnership's activities.

All these factors add up to a kind of enforced passivity on the part of the limited partner and a lack of room to maneuver your investment that might surprise, even shock someone who has had experience investing in stocks and bonds.

TAX BRACKETING: WHO CAN AFFORD SHELTERS?

If you are not at least in the 40 percent tax bracket and likely to remain so for a few years, this book may broaden your education, but it cannot be applied to your personal financial situation. Many tax advisers would be even more conservative, estimating that shelters are really useful only to those in the 50 percent bracket. Why? Because the shelter reduces your taxes by lowering your adjusted gross (or taxable) income. If your taxable income is in the 50 percent bracket, a 100 percent deductible tax shelter will actually only cost you fifty cents for every dollar invested, because under normal circumstances fifty cents of every dollar would have gone to pay taxes.

★ You may have heard that taxpayers in the 40 percent bracket can benefit by a specific class of tax shelters that offer rapid depreciation allowances. Be aware that continuing revisions of the tax code have reduced the depreciation allowances of those shelters.

As a matter of fact, your tax bracket does not apply to the whole of your income. The lowest part of your income is taxed at the lowest rate, the next highest at the next highest rate, and so on up the scale. A taxpayer in the 50 percent bracket is being taxed at that rate only on the highest level of income. Subtracting the amount you invest in a tax shelter from your taxable income will drop you to a lower tax bracket, as the following demonstrates:

Imagine a married couple filing jointly; they earn an annual income of $80,000. Let's assume that with the mortgage interest and real estate deductions their taxable income is about $60,000. How much would they save if they put $20,000 into a tax shelter that is 100 percent deductible?

Taxable income of $60,000 would be liable for a federal income tax of about $14,857 in 1985. Subtract the $20,000 tax shelter investment from the taxable income of $60,000, however, and the taxable income is only $40,000. Taxes due would be about $7,640. Subtract this lowered tax bill from what the couple would otherwise have owed and we find that the tax savings they reap is on the order of $7,217. In their tax bracket of 38 percent, they have spent only $12,783 in real dollars on their tax shelter investment of $20,000. They will make a profit down the line if the investment only earns

$12,784, but given an economically sound shelter, they should make considerably more than that on the $20,000 they have invested.

This couple has at once reduced their tax bill for the year and bought into an investment that, presumably, will be profitable. An investor in a lower tax bracket will gain less in tax benefits and may therefore find the shelter a less attractive investment. On the other hand, he or she will be acquiring an interest in a property by means of a transaction that is in part financed by the federal government.

★ This is as good a point as any to recall that Marlys Harris reported in *Money* magazine that at least one highly respected financial planner guesses that only 10 percent of the tax shelter proposals he sees annually are in fact good investment possibilities. The tax law is encouraging but not guaranteeing your investment in legitimate shelters.

To repeat: When you are figuring out just how attractive a tax shelter might be for you in your current financial situation, look at your taxable income *after* you have taken all your deductions and other income adjustments. In addition to understanding the benefits of altering your individual tax bracket by sheltering income, you must also understand the concept of "leveraging" and the use of what is called "depreciation."

DEPRECIATION: THE KEY TO MOST TAX SHELTERS

Although the full range of tax allowances and incentives includes tax credits and depletion deductions (to be discussed later), what makes most tax shelters work, what is most likely to earn you tax benefits, is depreciation. The theory is that all tangible or investment-related property has a finite and determinable "useful life." Therefore, the government will allow an enterprise to write off "a reasonable allowance for the exhaustion, wear and tear of property used in trade or business, or of property held for the production of income." In other words, the cost of a property can be written off in annual deductions taken over the useful life of the property in question.

★ There has been much activity recently in this area of the law, both in the machinations of the promoters and in the reexaminations of the law by the government's own tax experts. One feature of the 1984 revisions, for example, was to "stretch" the depreciation period for most real estate from fifteen to eighteen years, thereby extending the period during which deductions for depreciation of the property could be taken.

Starting in 1981, useful life of a property is determined arbitrarily by the tax code, in most cases under ACRS, or the accelerated cost recovery system. This aspect of the Economic Recovery Tax Act was an instrument of social policy, an attempt to encourage investment in selected areas of the nation's economy. Depreciable assets now have assigned lives of three, five, ten, fifteen or eighteen years known as cost recovery periods; the length of the cost recovery period depends upon the type of property being depreciated.

Also, the 1981 act made it more attractive to compute the depreciation of property by using the "accelerated method" rather than the "straight line method." With the latter, annual deductions for depreciation are equal, computed simply by dividing the cost of the property by the number of years of depreciation—say, $5,000 annually on a piece of business equipment considered to have a useful life of ten years and originally costing $50,000.

Under the accelerated method you are allowed to take larger deductions in the first years of the cost recovery period. This feature, combined with the relatively brief assigned lives now set down by the government, dramatically reduces the period during which the cost of business assets can be fully deducted. The piece of equipment with an actual useful life of a decade can perhaps be written off in half that time; also, the accelerated method can produce relatively large deductions in the first year of the purchase—very useful for the taxpayer who needs a large tax loss right away.

The depreciation of business equipment is a factor in some of the shelters to be described later. For right now, let's return to our sample couple and to an example of depreciation as it applies to a real estate investment. Remember, this imaginary couple has an imaginary income and tax situation—simple, in round numbers, predictable for the life of the example. This is not anything like reality, of course. The point is to make the concepts clear, so that you will understand the language of tax advisers and others skilled enough to deal with the real-life complications and imponderables of your actual situation. Before we let that couple earn their depreciations, though, we must discuss the "leveraging" concept.

LEVERAGING: A SWEETENING OF THE DEAL

To "leverage," in the world of tax shelters, means "to use someone else's money to invest in your tax shelter." Keeping our figures in round numbers, the sample couple could invest their $20,000 in a piece of real estate priced at $100,000, with the other $80,000 coming in the form of a loan from the bank. They would still deduct the $20,000 shelter investment from their acquired gross income, thereby putting themselves into the lower tax bracket, but now they can also benefit from depreciation and leveraging, receiving tax benefits from the total $100,000 investment even though only $20,000 of their own money is involved (and that, as you recall, was money being spent at fifty cents on the dollar). Using the straight line method of computing depreciation, the couple could declare a paper loss on the $100,000 real estate shelter of $5,555.55 annually, or one-eighteenth of the total purchase price. In addition, of course, they would deduct from taxable income the interest paid on the $80,000 mortgage to the bank.

In practice, these tax benefits would be computed by the general partner of the limited partnership, who would choose the method of computing depreciation, arrange the bank loan for financing the business venture, and, as we have seen, take the responsibility for ensuring that the tax shelter makes a profit in the long run. Each of the limited partners, then, would be sharing those benefits that accrue to our happily uncomplicated sample couple: 1) a tax rate reduction because of investing in the tax shelter deal; 2) a depreciation deduction, computed by whichever method the general partner has chosen; and 3) a deduction of mortgage interest against the income from the shelter.

Loud Warning Beeps

From the moment the deal is struck, the tax benefits described all decline in value to you the taxpayer. First of all, the investment amount itself is deducted from taxable income only in the year invested; the following year you have returned to the higher bracket, if your income has remained steady and you haven't found other avenues of tax relief. Second, the depreciation deductions may be higher in the first years of the venture than later on, according to the determination of the general partner. Third, there's the declining interest deduction, since interest payments are made on the unpaid balance of the mortgage, and that is being paid off. Finally, if the shelter is economically sound, it should begin to make money, probably in rental income.

Caution: The attractive tax losses at the inception of a shelter begin slowly melting away, particularly if the economy causes an increase in rental income or other profits.

Another warning, before you leap to too many conclusions: A real estate tax shelter is different from other types of deals. Perhaps the most important difference is that the at-risk rule of the tax code does not apply to real estate shelters, which constitute a majority of the government's efforts to encourage investment in the economy. It is because the at-risk rules do not apply here that our couple—who selected a real estate shelter—is not liable for the $80,000 loan taken out to finance their investment. Even though they can deduct the interest payments as if they really were at risk, as far as they and the other limited partners are concerned the loan will probably be what is called a "nonrecourse loan," one for which the general partner —but not they as limited partners—will be liable. This at-risk concept will be very important to the investor in shelters that are not involved with real estate, as we will see later.

★ Another fact of life about real estate shelters: Attractive as the possibility might seem, you cannot use the shelter concept for your own home. Depreciation applies only to property that is an investment or that is used in a business. The limitations are strict, and you should check with your accountant whenever you have a question; for example, a summer home bought as an investment for rental income and so depreciated can be used only rarely by members of your family and under certain restrictions.

DEPRECIATIONS: IS THERE NO LIMIT?

Until the enactment of the 1984 Tax Reform Act, promoters of certain shelters were smugly promising first-year tax loss ratios of four to one or even five to one. As you might expect, many of these schemes were immediately checked out by the IRS; most likely, investors lost the extraordinary tax benefits and faced back taxes along with penalty fees.

The Government Ideal

Let's take another look at what the government allows, in its own words. It's a good way of summing up what we have said so far about the tax shelter concept:

"There are three selling points that are common to most tax-shelter investments: (1) the ability to defer tax liability to a later year, (2) the opportunity to convert ordinary income to tax-favored income, such as capital gains, and (3) the use of borrowed funds to finance the investment (leverage)."

We will be discussing "capital gains" later; for now, just note that the three "selling points" mentioned by the government, and accepted by it, do not include rapine. To underscore the point, the law now requires that any shelter promising the investor a two to one or greater tax shelter ratio must be registered with the IRS—that is, made available for processing through the new improved computers of the agency. This law specifically applies to tax shelters that offer such ratios "as of the close of any of the first 5 years ending after the offering date."

You would be wise, therefore, to steer clear of shelters offering extraordinary write-offs. First, you may find that the shelter will be declared illegal by the IRS, through whose pre-filing notification system investors are warned not to claim specified write-offs at risk of audit, loss of deductions, imposition of interest and penalties, and the like. Second, such wild promises might indicate the moving presence of "a con." As of 1984, a new penalty will be imposed on any promoter who makes fraudulent statements about a tax shelter or grossly overvalues the worth of the enterprise: a $1,000 fine or one-fifth (previously one-tenth) of the promoter's gross income from the deal, whichever is greater. This is an added deterrent, but is it enough to protect you? Perhaps not. Some promoters are still willing to risk getting caught. The best protection for you is to aim to *defer, not avoid,* tax liability, aim to convert your taxable income into income which is liable to (the lower) capital gains taxes, and aim to take advantage of leveraging to increase your tax savings and your investment in the economy.

★ A good tax counselor would probably agree with the following statement made by an accountant in a western state, where shelter promoters have sometimes been extravagantly optimistic about their offerings and have preyed upon the moderately well fixed retirees who have moved west in search of sun and the easy life: "Like any reputable accountant, I'm happy to see the shysters attacked under the new IRS rules; I really am. The guys who don't follow the rules, who don't come up with deals that are true to the intent of Congress in making the laws about tax shelters, are making it that much harder on the rest of us. *And* they're making the taxpayer expect too much out of shelter activity."

TO SUM UP...

In this chapter we have introduced you to the tax shelter. Whether or not a tax shelter will be useful to you depends upon your tax bracket *and* upon your ability to leave an investment where it is for the life of the shelter. You are looking for short-term tax losses in combination with long-term real gains, in terms of cash accrual. You are looking for an economically sound investment, managed by professionals who have a personal stake in the success of the business venture and who are unlikely to eat unfairly into the profits with inflated fees and other charges. Essentially, you are judging the attractiveness of the tax shelter just as you would judge any other investment: Is it legitimate? Is it well managed? Does it have promise? Is it a worthwhile business venture rather than a hit-or-miss sweepstakes try?

In addition, you will want to know just exactly how beneficial leveraging and depreciation will be in your case. You may want the general partner of the business venture or your tax adviser to discuss with you the relative advantages of the straight line method or the accelerated method of depreciation. You will want to understand what the interest rate of leveraging will mean to your annual tax obligation as the term of the shelter continues over the years. Most of all, perhaps, you will want to have a clear understanding of the projected balance of income against loss from one year to the next. You will definitely want to know when your tax benefits end and the government begins to collect the taxes that have been deferred by your participation in the shelter.

In the next chapter we will begin to describe some popular tax shelters. Each will have its own advantages and disadvantages, its own specific legal requirements. We will also encounter some important terms, such as "recapture" and "capital gains."

5

SOME OF THE MOST COMMON SHELTERS—PART ONE

As we discuss a few of the most common types of tax shelters, you may be imagining each as a possibility for your own tax situation. The format of a shelter should not be the only consideration, however, as we are cautioned by Frank M. Robbins III, an investment counselor with Patten & Patten, Inc., in Chattanooga, Tennessee. "Since fairness really is the theme of continuing tax reform," Robbins says, "it is best to choose shelters which have an intrinsic value because they provide a useful service. They will be less vulnerable to attack from a commonsense standpoint, more likely to survive the whims of public policy if they have an obvious underlying usefulness." If Robbins is right, many of the shelters that seem most attractive purely on the basis of their structure might not, in the long run, have the "legs" or stamina that you really want for your investment.

NET-LEASED REAL ESTATE

In a net-lease shelter, the limited partnership can borrow the entire cost of a property, receive the full benefits of depreciation deductions, and, during the life of the deal, reap substantial tax savings for the limited partners, especially if they are in the 50 percent bracket.

How does it work? First, the promoter has to find a tenant with a credit rating and record of performance so strong that any bank will be happy to make a mortgage loan for the full value of the property. Obviously, few companies or corporations are in such a prestigious position; a net-lease shelter will more than likely involve a tenant with a very well known name. In addition, the tenant must agree to undertake all the maintenance and operation of the leased property—an unconditional responsibility. The tenant will pay rent that covers the cost of the mortgage payments, and little or nothing more than that; in other words, in exchange for the opportunity to gain large depreciation and interest deductions for their participation in the shelter, the limited partners are willing to accept little or no cash return. Finally, the deal will probably include the proviso that after the lease expires (and, simultaneously, the mortgage is paid off), the tenant will have the option of deciding to extend its use of the property for a second period (say, twenty to thirty years)—at a reduced rent. This reduction, in fact, may be as much as half the rent paid during the term of the original lease.

You can probably see where the difficulties arise. At first the shelter is beneficial for people who need tax losses. But, as we discussed in the previous chapter, the benefits eventually diminish and the investors then find themselves confronted with an adverse tax situation. Remember the warning about burnout? Once the deductions are used up (for most properties these days, after the eighteenth year of the deal), the rental income, which had previously been used to cover the mortgage payment, becomes taxable income. That is, the interest deductions have become insignificant as the mortgage is paid off. What had been a substantial rent paid by a corporation for a large property, but giving tax benefits, becomes simply...a substantial rent that is taxable. Put another way, the deal reaches a crossover point, and the limited partners who were gaining the benefits of tax losses are rather suddenly faced with annual tax liabilities.

Of course, the wise investor, responsive to good tax advice, would have been investing some or all of the tax savings in anticipation of the crossover point.

There is another possible solution—to sell the property, at

which time the profits earned by the limited partners can be taxed at the lower capital gains rates.

CAPITAL GAINS: SOMETIMES AN OPTION

First, one of our favorite warnings: There may be changes afoot in the treatment of capital gains. As of this writing, however, only 40 percent of your profit is subject to tax, if it is considered a capital gain; for example, if you have earned $10,000 that is considered capital gains, only $4,000 will be taxed—and it will be taxed at your tax bracket rate. If that were 50 percent, then your tax liability would be only $2,000—20 percent of the $10,000 earnings. In other words, you would benefit from one of the "tax preferences" allowed by the IRS, a preferential treatment that results in the "exclusion" of 60 percent of your earnings from taxes.

★ This tax preference may trigger the AMT, or alternative minimum tax, in some situations. This tax is discussed on page 40.

It is not necessarily true, however, that the earnings of a net-lease shelter are exactly the same as cash profit; the transaction may show what is called a "phantom gain." Here's why:

Assume that the leased property in the net-lease shelter was originally bought for $10 million. Over the eighteen-year depreciation period, the cost of the building on the property could be depreciated (say, $9 million); the cost of the land itself ($1 million, our example) cannot be depreciated, however, under our tax code. This undepreciated amount is known as the "adjusted basis" of the property. If investors in this net-lease shelter wanted to get out of the deal at the crossover point and were able to sell the property for the original cost of $10 million, it might look as if no gains were made. In fact, the gain works out to be $10 million minus the undepreciated $1 million; the limited partners have earned $9 million on the deal when their accumulated deductions have been taken into account. Under capital gains treatment, 60 percent of these earnings would be (assuming that each limited partner is indeed in the 50 percent bracket) half of $3,600,000 (40 percent of $9 million)—a tax liability of $1,800,000.

Would the limited partnership then receive a cash profit of $7,200,000 (gains of $9 million minus the capital gains tax of $1,800,000)? No. Most likely, a mortgage is still being held on the property, since the original net-lease shelter and mortgage were probably set up for at least twenty-five years, perhaps longer. The balance of that mortgage must be paid off. After eighteen years, the unpaid principal balance might be about $8 million. The limited partnership would realize an actual cash profit of $2 million—enough to pay off the capital gains taxes ($1,800,000) but with only a little bit left over ($200,000).

But could the property still sell for $10 million? Remember, it has been in use for eighteen years, probably suffering some wear and tear and loss of market appeal, no matter how conscientiously the tenant has managed it; moreover, the property carries with it the option mentioned previously—that the corporate tenant has the right to stay on at a reduced rent when the lease expires. The limited partnership might be fortunate, even considering the likelihood that the actual value of the land has appreciated over the years, to find a buyer willing to put up top dollar for a property that is likely to yield below-market rental income for twenty or thirty years.

The moral of the net-lease shelter, then, may be no different from the moral of all tax shelter activity: Look into the future, insofar as it is possible, when you invest; prepare for the crossover point.

REAL ESTATE: ALWAYS THE SALT OF THE EARTH?

For every beloved fairy tale of the financial world there's a horror story or two, but real estate has seemed to be the exception in this country in recent decades. Popular magazines and cocktail party gossip, front-page stories of the financial sections of major newspapers and television profiles—all have documented the runaway successes of entrepreneurs and the steady but significant gains of the homeowner in most markets.

Even in real estate, however, there have recently been some unwelcome surprises. Many a Southern California homeowner saw property values decline alarmingly a couple of years ago; farmers in many parts of the country have been told that their land has declined 50 percent in market value, and even the most attractive, well-built middle-class housing can drop in value overnight when a major plant nearby closes down, if it is crucial to the area's economy. These may be exceptions, but the investor in real estate shelters should remember that nothing is predictable. People only lose money in "sure things" because they only invest in "sure things" (at least in their own eyes).

Perhaps we should look at real estate in general, from the point of view of the highly cautious investor.

Are Real Estate Syndications Worry-Free?

The shelters offered by large real estate syndicates are likely to be characterized by diversity and reach, stressing either tax loss or income or a little of both. Wall Street, quite naturally, has not been insensitive to investor interest in the typically escalating real estate market or to taxpayer interest in tax shelters. Nevertheless, some experts warn that such syndicates do not necessarily offer everything you might want: a few years of sheltered income after some substantial deductions in the beginning, topped off with good capital gains later on.

For one thing, "sure things" can collapse. Who is moving into (or out of) an area? For how long? Why? Such questions—in other words, the dimensions of the human factor—are critically important in real estate, and the answers are not always immediately obvious. Everyone knows of projected developments, hailed by businessman and politician alike, that have failed miserably, perhaps for some intangible reason; and everyone has surely heard of real estate explosions that seem almost to have taken off on their own.

A good word for major real estate investment is "volatility." Just think of the cracked asphalt of the parking lot of the shopping center that went bust near your house; chances are that's a sight most people have seen. What happened? Did the neighborhood change? Was the management of the property inexpert or too casual? Perhaps the real estate syndicate paid too high a price or charged rents that were too high for the area. Was the syndicate more concerned about properties in another part of the country? These are all real possibilities, inherent in the nature of real estate management and speculation, and increasingly likely to occur when a syndicate is trying to handle properties that are very different from one another and widely scattered physically.

Evade "Recapture"

In certain cases the capital gains treatment of earnings from a real estate deal is not allowed: the tax benefits from the depreciation deductions (including the recent accelerated method of depreciation deductions) are "recaptured" by taxing portions of the gains at the investor's tax rate. Put another way, the accelerated deductions will have been subtracted from the original cost, lowering the adjusted basis of the property. Consequently, the taxable gain, or the difference between the adjusted basis and the price at which the partnership sells the property, will be greater, and this gain may be recaptured as ordinary income.

Obviously, recapture is a less appealing tax situation. The rules of recapture vary with the type of property involved; for example, low-income housing projects receive favorable recapture treatment (after 16⅔ years of ownership, capital gains treatment will be afforded any gain on the sale of the property). In general, recapture is more likely when a limited partnership uses accelerated depreciation to get large annual deductions in the first years of the deal. For example, when residential real estate is sold, there may be a significant difference between the deductions taken with the accelerated method and what would have been allowed up to that point by the straight line method; the difference is taxed at income tax rates. The amount recaptured as ordinary income is greater if the property is not residential realty.

As your tax adviser can explain when appropriate, you should probably choose a deal that takes maximum accelerated cost recovery methods only if you also have other shelter activities lined up to help you later on, when it's time to sell the property. Once again, foresight is recommended.

Someone Else's Troubles

There's no "lemon law" about used tax shelters, so the best advice is to stay away from them. Why, indeed, would one limited partnership sell out to another? Because the business venture is losing money. Why would the other limited partnership be willing to buy? In the hope of maximizing write-offs by incorporating the losses of the failing partnership. The problem is that the government is likely to see this scheme for what it is—a deal made entirely in the pursuit of tax loss, lacking both cash flow and the potential for profit somewhere down the line.

The Virtue of Patience

Despite the Sunday supplement stories of overnight success in real estate deals, the real estate investor must have patience, along with the understanding that real estate is optimally approached as a long-term investment. As we have seen, recapture looms ominously when a property is sold too early in the term of a tax shelter deal. In addition, a limited partner will probably have difficulty selling his interest in a shelter (an option usually given only with the agreement of the other limited partners), since much of the tax advantages will have been exhausted up front.

Ideally, two factors will occur over the first ten to fifteen years of a deal to reward investor patience: a decrease in the unpaid principal balance of the mortgage and an increase in the market value of the property. This combination should make the property attractive enough so that a profit can be made by outright sale, refinancing, or sale of a partner's interest.

When Alarms Should Sound

1. Have your tax adviser, lawyer, or accountant help you evaluate the properties included in a real estate tax shelter; the promised tax benefits will never materialize if the cost projections are hopelessly out of line.

2. Be wary of tax shelters that lump together real estate and other kinds of businesses; to succeed, such deals would require a rather remarkable (and unlikely) breadth of experience and expertise on the part of the general partner involved.

3. Gaze intently at the deal and promoter from all possible angles. Are nondeductible fees being imposed? Is the general partner getting a commission before you earn something on your investment? Are there possible conflicts of interest because the promoter has affiliations with some party to the venture?

4. Think twice about the promises of a so-called blind pool syndicate or tax shelter, which does not list specific properties but promises to select the best investments possible after the money is raised; how can the tax advantages of properties that are not yet chosen be known in advance?

Foreclosure, or Insult Added to Injury

Even in the unfortunate event of a mortgage foreclosure on tax-sheltered property, there is still the possibility of a tax on "gain." At foreclosure, the law says that the investor has received, in effect, an amount equal to the unpaid principal balance of the mortgage loan. Serious tax problems could result, unless the permanent mortgage loan is refinanced so that ownership of the property is retained and the potential for profit in the future is enhanced.

MINIMUM TAXES

Earlier we described capital gains tax treatment as a kind of "tax preference." To balance this and other tax preferences, the government has designed a minimum tax to ensure that well-heeled taxpayers with wily investment plans do not end up paying little or no tax. This leveling mechanism is the "alternative minimum tax," which can come as an unpleasant surprise to the taxpayer.

In general this tax is triggered by excess deductions for depreciation. The alternative minimum tax is based upon the taxpayer's "alternative minimum taxable income," which is adjusted gross income increased by tax preference items such as the long-term capital gains deduction of 60 percent and excess deductions, minus certain itemized deductions. This alternative minimum tax is imposed, moreover, only when it is greater than the taxpayer's regular income tax liability. These are matters that should be discussed in detail with a tax adviser if there is a likelihood that either of these taxes will be imposed.

A REVIEW OF THE BASICS

In spite of warnings about the possible perils, real estate investment is the most popular type of venture. It is tangible, which for some investors carries an emotional appeal, and it is likely to appreciate over the long run. Furthermore, as we have seen, this type of investment is encouraged by the law, despite the recent public statement of a high government official that "we shouldn't have incentives in tax policy."

Real estate is the only type of tax-sheltered investment that can be purchased with a nonrecourse loan, thereby evading the at-risk rules of the tax code. In certain instances it offers such substantial excess deductions that income tax liability can be virtually eliminated. As shelter ventures should, real estate is likely to produce cash returns. And, although we have not discussed them, there are often a great many so-called soft costs, which can be deducted as soon as they are paid (in contrast with hard costs, like the cost of equipment, which are only recoverable under ACRS—the accelerated cost recovery system). Soft costs include real estate taxes, the interest being paid on the mortgage loan, and those business expenses that the IRS will allow as "ordinary and necessary" (such as utilities, for example, and other expenses of daily operation).

Although we have not yet emphasized the point, you should attempt to balance all the projected expenses and expected profits of a real estate deal. Is the rental income high enough? Is the occupancy rate high enough, and likely to remain so? Is the depreciation method being used the one that's best for your individual tax situation? Is your tax bracket likely to remain high enough for the next few years to take advantage of the tax benefits of the shelter? Similarly, have you set enough money aside, or do you have other resources adequate enough, so that you will not have to try to liquidate your shelter investment in a hurry? Unfortunately, we all too often assume that the future is unlikely to bring a sudden setback in our economic circumstances. Optimism is healthy, and often justified, but it is also important that one not make investments based upon unrealistic expectations about the future. It is only reasonable to expect that your economic situation may be radically different over the next few years. In any case, make sure that all your speculations about the future get the benefit of another opinion, preferably a schooled and professional one. And don't fall prey to the illusion of time. A tax bill that will be due at the crossover point of some deal may seem a long way off; at that point, however, it will be due *right now.*

Don't expect miracles from real estate shelters; just as your investment is gradually appreciating over the long term, you must be building up, gradually and faithfully, whatever nest egg will be necessary to meet the obligations of the future, whether taxable as income or as capital gains.

LOW-INCOME HOUSING

Government-assisted housing projects may be an attractive tax shelter, no matter what your political feelings about federal subsidies to housing. Such projects, generally initiated to provide housing for low-income families, offer the investor benefits not available in other types of real estate, even though the law restricts the investor's actual cash return to a low 2 or 3 percent of cash investment. First, there is the unusually attractive leverage offered by the government: a forty-year mortgage loan that will cover up to 85 percent of the cost of the property. Second, the depreciation deductions are unusually rapid; in the first five years of the deal, about half the cost of the property can be depreciated, using the accelerated method. Third, the annual deductions for mortgage interest are relatively substantial for about the first half of the mortgage period, because the term is so long. Fourth, the government offers liberal recapture and capital gains treatment, if the property is held for at least one hundred months. These features to the side, it is possible that the up-front write-offs on subsidized housing projects can work out to more than twice or three times the amount of cash you invested.

But Wait

In this type of housing, many of the tenants will be receiving monthly rent subsidies from the government, based upon need. As tenants begin to make more money, however, they lose their eligibility for subsidies. To some experts, therefore, it seems likely that the turnover in such projects will be high. The rapid turnover, of course, is a constant drain on management. More important, however, unoccupied apartments mean less cash flow to investors in the shelter; and it is likely that year-round occupancy of more than 95 percent will be necessary to make the deal work, with tenants paying rent when due. Finally, the tax benefits of these projects bring on special problems:

1. The cost of the property might be inflated, because the appeal to some investors of the large up-front deductions is so strong.

2. For all the wisdom of government bureaucrats, a particular project might be located in an area where it is unnecessary or in a neighborhood where property values are on the decline.

3. Promoters of this type of deal sometimes charge unusually large fees to applicants for the limited partnership.

4. The IRS and the general partner may have different ideas about the depreciation period for the property.

5. Should the deal fail, the gains of the investors will be recaptured—a paper gain based upon the cost of the original mortgage, not upon the assessed value of the bankrupt project.

Consider these factors when you find yourself attracted to the very real, and very legitimate, tax benefits to be found in the subsidized-housing tax shelter.

THE INVESTMENT TAX CREDIT

Investors in rehabilitation shelters are entitled to an investment tax credit, an amount related to the age and (when appropriate) historical value of the building to be renovated. The distinctive feature of a tax credit, it should be noted, is that the amount of the credit is subtracted directly from the taxpayer's income tax. The other tax benefits we have been discussing, you will recall, are subtracted from the taxpayer's taxable income, or adjusted gross income, thereby lowering the amount of income and rate of taxation. By contrast, the investment tax credit reduces the amount of the tax bill itself.

Old, but Not Vintage

There is a tax credit of 20 percent (that is, one-fifth) of the cost of rehabilitation for a structure at least forty years old, if it is to be used as a commercial property. If the building is at least thirty years old, the credit allowed is 15 percent of the expenses of rehabilitation. In either case, the remaining costs of rehabilitation (80 or 85 percent) have to be recovered in no less than 15 or 18 years (depending on acquisition date), using the straight line method of depreciation.

★ The eligibility of a property for this special tax credit depends upon the use to which it will be put after rehabilitation; in other words, no matter what the purpose of the original structure, it can qualify if it will ultimately be used for commercial purposes.

A larger tax credit of 25 percent is available for the rehabilitation of buildings that are considered "historic," no matter what the projected use of the structure after the rehabilitation. In these cases the building has to be approved by a state or local preservation board, located in a "historic district," and deemed integral to that district, or it has to be listed as a nationally significant historic property in the National Register.

To qualify for the 15 percent, 20 percent, or 25 percent credit, rehabilitation expenses over a two-year period (ending with the current year) must exceed the greater of $5,000 or the adjusted basis of the structure.

★ Fifty percent of the historic structure credit must be subtracted from the owner's basis; by contrast, the entire tax credit of 15 percent or 20 percent on older properties renovated for commercial purposes must be subtracted from the basis of the building.

Be warned that older structures may require substantial renovation to become commercially viable. Whether you convert to apartments or to office space, your tenants may demand certain amenities that cannot be conveniently added to an historic property; in addition, there may be restrictions on the type of renovation allowed—it may be very expensive to restore a facade, for example, or to replace columns in a way deemed appropriate by local preservationists.

Finally, there are some factors to be considered in any commercial property investment, whether rehabilitated or built from the ground up:

1. The longer leases of commercial buildings may give income stability to the investor, but in the event of a surge in real estate values they cannot be raised quickly to market levels.

2. The tenants of a commercial building are less likely than apartment dwellers to move often, therefore guaranteeing low vacancy rates, but the needs of commercial tenants may be so specialized that the property will require extensive management time and expertise.

3. The rate of return on your investment may not be as high as in other types of property, but the acquisition of a well-known and highly successful commercial tenant may give you security over the long term.

4. As in any tax shelter activity, check out the qualifications of the management: experienced? forthcoming with you? trusted by previous tenants? committed to the property?

IN CLOSING, SOME WORDS TO REMEMBER

Capital Gains Treatment: A tax preference that allows you to exclude 60 percent of your gains from taxation; generally speaking, it applies only to gains from property that you or your partnership have held for at least six months.

Depreciation: The tax deduction you take over a specific period of time for costs deemed depreciable. Two methods can be used to compute your depreciations, either the straight line method or the accelerated method.

Minimum Taxes: The alternative minimum tax, designed to keep you from paying less than a "fair share" of taxes in a year when you have an excess of tax benefits, such as huge up-front losses on depreciation.

Nonrecourse Loan: A mortgage for which you are not liable, although the general partner of the limited partnership in which you participate will be.

Recapture: The government's device for collecting some of the taxes you have been allowed to defer over the life of a tax sheltered business venture. Your gain from a sale (or, in certain cases, part of it) will be subject to taxation at your ordinary income tax rates.

KEEP YOUR EYES OPEN

Sometimes a promoter will really dazzle you with a specific tax shelter deal, and your own good common sense might become clouded. This can happen with a solid-sounding real estate deal as easily as it can with the more exotic methods of sheltering income. Don't be afraid of taking tried-and-true, boring advice. Listen to the professionals you have hired to help you: lawyer, tax counselor, or accountant. Give a reasonable amount of attention each day to business news; you'll be amazed at how much you can learn about property in your area by looking through the local section of the paper, from who's building where to who is facing bankruptcy and why. Don't hesitate to ask questions, no matter how apparently unsophisticated; an honest and capable tax shelter promoter has every reason to help you understand the deal (for one thing, he certainly does not want to have you develop expectations that will prove unrealistic and may possibly provoke a lawsuit). Make tax planning a part of your ongoing life, not a hasty, hectic activity for the twilight of the year, when the best deals are gone (besides, deals entered into from October on are likely to seem questionable in intent to the Internal Revenue Service).

6

SOME OF THE MOST COMMON SHELTERS—PART TWO

In this chapter we'll focus on two types of shelters, the increasingly popular leasing of equipment and the romantic (in the eyes of many investors) world of oil and gas. And we'll end with a look at the rapidly changing area of research and development, a field likely to be favored by the government for some time because, in the words of a treasury official, "there is momentum for high technology; it's evil to be against high technology."

EQUIPMENT LEASING

Tax shelters in equipment leasing seem to fall midway in the adventure spectrum: not quite as daring as oil and gas, but not always as reliable as real estate. This may be a matter of perception. Although the nation's recent efforts to upgrade industry to meet increased foreign competition have fueled investment in this type of shelter activity, there has not yet been enough time to establish a track record. In any event, some experts feel that equipment leasing will become the most desirable shelter of the coming decade, although there are many questions to be asked. It does not require a lot of money to participate in equipment leasing shelters. In most cases it will not be difficult to finance the deal. Finally, there is the strong likelihood that a good income and, eventually, a capital gain will be generated.

How It Works

First of all, remember that we have moved out of the nonrecourse world of real estate mortgages. To satisfy the at-risk rules of the IRS, you will be fully liable for any loan required to purchase the equipment being leased, and you will have to put down at least 20 percent of the total purchase price in cash. The lease must end on or before the point at which 80 percent of the "useful life" of the equipment has been exhausted; and when the lease term ends, the projected fair market value of the equipment should be at least 20 percent of the price you paid in the beginning. As you can see, the conditions are meant to ensure that you and your limited partners in an equipment leasing tax shelter want to make money on the deal as well as reap tax benefits. To that end, your lessor will not be given the option of buying the equipment from you at prices lower than fair market value. The lessor cannot guarantee your loan or help you financially with the purchase, either by paying for part of the equipment or by lending you money.

When your limited partnership buys the equipment (be it oil tankers, medical equipment, computers, farm machinery, or jet planes), it is immediately leased out at a rental rate that will, optimally, cover the loan payments and also earn cash to be distributed among you and your limited partners. The question to be answered before this deal is struck probably occurred to you when you first heard of equipment leasing: Precisely why would the "user," or the lessor, want to lease equipment rather than purchase it?

Balancing the Risk-Benefit Ratio

There are very good reasons, as it happens, why a sound, reputable company would want to lease your equipment. Perhaps the first is to spend less money: the lessor gets to use equipment that has been fully financed without having to invest any money of his own, and can therefore reduce his capital expenditure. In some cases, as a matter of fact, it may well be that the company, though promising, just isn't able to raise the money for a down payment on the equipment. This is not necessarily a danger signal for you, although you should certainly determine that the company does not have a bad credit rating. It may be that the firm is so young and untried that banks have better reason for skepticism than you might.

Another reason for a company to lease is the deductibility of lease payments as an ongoing business expense. Repayment of the loan, or amortization, brings no tax benefits. Third, the company may have its eye on establishing a long-term relationship with your limited partnership as a possible source of investment monies for future needs. Lastly, the cost of leasing equipment may be lower than the cost of buying, since you and your limited partners might be able to live with a lower rate of return on your investment than a lending institution would accept.

Set against the advantages to the lessor, what are your benefits? Essentially, you are receiving relatively modest earnings for a fairly short period of time (depending, of course, upon the type of equipment and its useful life). Most tax experts would agree that equipment leasing is a fairly conservative type of shelter. There is, of course, the possibility that your lessor will default on the lease, and you should therefore insist on a guarantee of your claim to the equipment, a "perfected security interest" designed to protect the priority of your claim over that of any other creditors. You should make every effort to avoid this situation, however, since it can be very difficult to find a new lessor for used equipment.

Still, the tax benefits are attractive enough for you to take the reasonable risks of this type of shelter. You will be able to deduct the interest on the loan for the purchase of the equipment, and you can deduct the depreciation of the equipment at an accelerated rate. It is possible, though not all that likely, that your partnership can take advantage of the 10 percent investment tax credit (because of certain restrictions, this credit only applies when buying and leasing railroad cars).

As for the income, some experts believe that a sound equipment leasing shelter, properly structured, can yield an annual return of at least 8 percent.

★ As the promoter of your deal will certainly know, since he or she will want to keep the management responsibilities of your shelter deal to a minimum, it is best to set up the lease so that the lessor has the responsibility of maintaining and supplying the equipment being leased.

What to Look Out For

Remember that equipment leases will be short-term. After all, your lessor wants top-of-the-line, up-to-date equipment, probably to keep pace with the latest technological innovations; the user will not want to be stuck with obsolescent equipment, particularly in business where new "generations" of equipment are produced every few years. Also, you will reach burnout rather quickly; consequently, phantom gain may become a tax problem if you do not adequately prepare. According to Robert and Carol Tannhauser, authors of *Tax Shelters: A Complete Guide,* the relatively early crossover point is probably the most serious drawback of equipment leasing tax shelters.

Trouble Down the Line?

Be sure that you keep abreast of government attitudes toward equipment leasing shelters. It's the old story: as more investors (and their brokers) recognize the attractions of equipment leasing, the IRS grows more interested in what is going on. Can so many investors really be standing in line for the privilege of taking risks? Even if you put up the money, for example, is there really that much risk when the lessor is extremely reliable, the equipment essential, and the business involved likely to make a good profit? Could your deal be seen by the IRS as, in effect, an installment sale agreement, by means of which your limited partnership is transferring ownership of the equipment to the user? That might very well be the agency's position, if you cannot establish that you indeed have a substantial economic interest in the deal.

★ The various restrictions on equipment leasing that we have discussed are the government's *guidelines,* not law. They are designed to define an area of activity within which you and your limited partners are most likely to be assuming the risks, burdens, and benefits of owning the equipment. To be certain that your shelter will be considered legitimate, you might want to request an advance ruling from the IRS as to whether the deal will be seen as a lease agreement or a sales agreement. You will certainly want to discuss the possibility of an adverse ruling with your tax adviser.

A final note about equipment leasing. Clearly the best investment will be in equipment that is demanded by growth industries. In other words, you and your promoter will not be considering the equipment itself in isolation from the condition of the overall economy; for instance, it might not be sensible to invest in the most advanced equipment for refining crude oil when there is an oil glut. You must understand the nature of the business that wants to use your equipment. You should probably be aware of government policies. Recently, for example, a major newspaper speculated that the government is shifting "the use of taxes to promote economic development and growth...from giving priority to aiding the so-called smokestack industries...to aiding the growth of high-technology industries." It's extremely important to have this kind of general information, along with specific data about the industry in which your potential lessor is involved, in order to maximize the likelihood of success for your shelter. While you needn't assign yourself the impossible task of becoming an instant expert, you should at least ensure that your promoter understands the business that will use the equipment your limited partnership will lease.

TO SUM UP...

Remember that with equipment leasing shelters, the significant benefits of accelerated depreciation are balanced by the rapidity with which crossover will occur. Remember, too, that you should not become so tantalized by the attractive tax losses that you forget the necessity of getting an economic return at the termination of lease (remaining useful life of the equipment), if not during it. And for those who might encounter the problem, make sure that the tax benefits of equipment leasing do not suddenly trigger the tax liability of the alternative minimum tax.

OIL AND GAS SHELTERS

At last we get to sex appeal. Something about oil and gas shelters seduces the otherwise sensible investor, can wind him or her in the coils of what can often resemble passion; then, not all that infrequently, it loses its mysterious attraction overnight and leaves behind little but disillusionment, disappointment, and a dazed feeling.

Nevertheless, there are certain straightforward, rational points to be made about these types of shelters. As you will see, some investments are riskier than others. Also, you must learn a few more technical terms in order to understand the specifics of an oil or gas venture. There are dangers peculiar to these shelters, from the risk that you will buy an "alligator" (an investment that just eats up your money without ever giving any return) to the possibility that the IRS will take an unusual interest in your income tax return. But you probably shouldn't even think about investing in oil or gas shelters unless a part of you fantasizes about running away from home to become a riverboat gambler. These investments do not promote sound sleep. To quote Robert L. Nessen, author of *More Money Now,* "If you are anything like me, with a faint heart when it comes to investing money, you are going to be hurtled past your threshold of pain by the uncertainty of oil and gas."

OIL: IS IT STILL BLACK GOLD?

As this book is being written, world oil prices are dropping. A trend? An aberration? For the answer, you might look at the experts' columns in the business magazines, where you'll probably find a fairly wide range of forecasts. Still, no one expects that oil exploration will soon become a vain and unprofitable enterprise; it's just that in the near future earnings may diminish and the government may become less interested in encouraging investment in the field. There might also be a decline in the dangerously high expectations all too many investors have.

In any case, it is currently estimated that production throughout the world will be dramatically insufficient within the next fifteen years or so; therefore, those in the industry with foresight are striving to find new sources of oil and gas. With luck and caution, your tax shelter might be the beneficiary of improved technology, good long-range planning, and sensible expectation—*if* you stay away from the deals that promise amazingly high returns on your investment (or, in fact, "promise" anything at all). Seriously consider these sobering statistics: Most in the industry agree that the chance of discovering a reservoir that can be exploited commercially is about fifty to one. (Compare this with the success probabilities in real estate or equipment leasing shelters.) It is not difficult to see why such activity is called "wildcatting." Nor is it surprising that the typical tax consultant will probably discourage all but the most financially secure investors from trying out oil and gas shelters.

SOME IMPORTANT TERMS: TRADE LANGUAGE

There are two types of drilling, a tribute to the unpredictability of the business (remember: No one *knows* what's really down there or —even more important, perhaps—whether or not it can profitably be brought up). The wildcat well is called an "exploratory well," drilled on land that is relatively untested, although somebody believes there is good reason to suspect that it will produce oil. Beware anyone who tries to interest you in such drilling, unless they admit that the chance of success is slight; this kind of investment has been likened to roulette. The "developmental well," drilled very close to productive wells already in existence, is much more likely to produce. According to one expert, developmental drilling, in the proper hands, is likely to produce as many as three wells for every four drilling attempts—not bad odds, although we shall see that the discovery of oil does not necessarily guarantee the investment's success financially. Still, if things work out reasonably well, your limited partnership will make back the original investment in about four years and, possibly, double that amount in another five or six years.

Whichever well comes in for you, you have to be prepared for "assessments," the additional contributions to the deal that will be necessary to pay for completion and production costs. In some deals the general partner may agree in the beginning to take responsibility for operating funds. More than likely, however, you and the other limited partners will be required to share whatever costs arise; if you do not contribute, you will forfeit all or part of your interest in the shelter. How much should be set aside for completion and production costs? Your general partner should have ballpark figures, of course, and you can check out the reasonableness of these with your accountant. In the drilling industry, however, the unpredictable is predictable. Not every well will suffer strikes, explosions, damaged equipment, foul weather, and the like... but yours might encounter one or more of these mishaps. The gambling aspect of oil and gas continues even after a "strike."

Usually your venture takes place on land owned by someone else. The right of your limited partnership to drill is given by lease. There may be an up-front "bonus payment" to the owner of the property; the agreement will include royalty payments to him or her, in the event that production actually begins, and perhaps rental payments ("delay rental") until that time. Naturally, you will want to know what is entailed by the lease agreement on your venture. It will therefore cost more money to become involved in developmental drilling than in an exploratory venture, and consequently your earnings are going to be less in a developmental drill—in spite of the fact that the odds of finding oil are more favorable. It's slightly less risky business. (Those with a hefty appetite for risk, though, can remind themselves that the greater the chance of loss, the greater the reward—if and when the exploratory well gushes.)

★ It is possible, by the way, to aim for the best of both worlds by investing in a balanced program that includes both types of drilling. Of course, when you aim for the middle, you avoid both extremes, both the disastrous loss and the big killing.

Look Out for the Payout

Learn the difference between the two basic methods of payout, or return of the investment, to the limited partners. Payout begins when the revenues grow larger than the costs of drilling and production. If there is a sharing arrangement of payout on a well-to-well basis, the limited partner in the deal is at a disadvantage. According to this scheme, the general partner can return a percentage of your money when one or a few wells begin to make a profit, and then take a larger share of the profits for himself or herself, perhaps as much as 50 percent. If the payout is on a program basis, however, all your contributions to the limited partnership will be returned before the larger cut for the general partner is triggered. Up until payout, by the way, the limited partners should be receiving almost the total amount of the revenues produced by the well or wells.

A SHELTER THAT HAS TO MAKE MONEY

You will notice that the emphasis here has been on the profits you should be seeking in oil and gas shelters, not on the tax benefits. In fact, the tax benefits are much less than in such shelters as real estate. For instance, it is unlikely that you will be getting the benefits of leverage. Most oil and gas shelters are cash investments, so the tax losses you claim cannot be greater than the actual amount invested. On the other hand, there is the benefit of "intangible drilling costs," which can be deducted in the first year of the investment. In oil and gas ventures, the costs of such tangible property as machinery, pipes, and casing are treated as capital expenditures, recoverable under ACRS (the accelerated cost recovery system). Intangible costs, however, which may rise as high as 75 percent of the total cost of the venture, are deductible in the year paid if the oil or gas well is "spudded" (drilling starts) in the year of payment or within ninety days after the end of the year. Intangible costs are such things as wages, fuel, repairs, and so forth, used in preparing the well site for drilling, in constructing the physical structures necessary to the operation, and in actually drilling the well. Since these activities are unlikely to produce income in the first year of the shelter deal, the limited partners will probably receive substantial deductions to their taxable income.

★ You must be extremely careful about taking deductions for expenses that are paid for, but do not actually occur, in the year you claim them. For example, your limited partnership might prepay the contractor for the drilling project before the end of the year, even though drilling will not start until the following year. To the IRS, this might look like a method of payment designed solely to reap desperately needed year-end tax benefits. A prepayment is deductible only if the well is spudded within 90 days after the close of the taxable year. The deduction is generally limited to an investor's cash investment. Your partnership will have to show that there is a valid economic purpose for the prepayment, such as the guarantee of a good price or the use of a specific drilling rig. Your general partner, of course, should be aware of this pitfall.

There are other considerations in oil and gas deals that should be discussed with your tax adviser. For example, it is legal for the deductions of a limited partner to be maximized by means of special allocations; that is to say, if the general partner agrees the entire amount of intangible drilling costs can be assigned to the limited partners, in effect allocating all the deductions to them. These arrangements have to be carefully written, however, and your adviser will alert you to situations that might lead to a conflict of interest.

Another special problem may occur if the well proves dry yet there is a gain on the disposition of property involved. According to the Tax Reform Act of 1976, such a gain could be taxed at your ordinary income tax rates rather than receive capital gains treatment, if the total of the deductions for intangible costs is greater than your total deductions would have been if you had used the depletion deduction.

This brings us, at last, to ''depletion,'' which is another incentive for the investor whose well strikes oil that is profitably brought out of the ground and profitably sold on the market. In other words, it's not guaranteed to you just because you invest in an oil or gas shelter.

Depletion—Depreciation by Another Name

In a sense, the depletion deduction is a form of depreciation, on the theory that as the operation of your well continues, the reserves in the ground are depreciating. In contrast with the depreciation deduction, however, depletion is not subject to recapture when you realize a gain on your property. You have to find oil, of course, for depletion to apply; a supply of mineral must actually be depleted. You also have to sell the oil or gas. Given those two prerequisites, you can set yourself up for a sizable benefit.

An extra fillip of the depletion deduction is that it is not based on the amount you have invested: it is a percentage of your gross income from the operation. It is possible, with a very successful well, that your depreciation benefit will exceed the amount of your investment. In 1983, the depletion allowance you could exclude from taxes was 16 percent of your gross income; in 1984, it was lowered to 15 percent, still a substantial tax-free cash return when a shelter does well. (Some readers may recall that previous to 1983 the percentage was 18 percent.)

There are limitations on depletion. First, there are two methods of computing the allowance: cost depletion and percentage depletion. Your accountant will compute your allowance each year using both methods, then apply the greater allowance of the two—but the amount cannot exceed 50 percent of the taxable income on the property, nor can it exceed 65 percent of your total taxable income in any one year.

THE HUMAN FACTOR: WHAT MAKES YOUR COLLEAGUES TICK?

Your oil or gas venture will probably lease property from a landowner who will have nothing to do with the operation. His role is clear: he will earn a guaranteed income during the search for oil, with the opportunity of making a good percentage should the well earn profits. However, what about the others involved with you and your limited partners? You should look closely at the qualifications and, above all, the motives of those who will be part of the deal.

You and your fellow investors will probably have had little contact with the oil or gas business. The promoter, the general partner, may also have had little direct experience of drilling operations, geological studies, and other practical aspects of the business, although he should know something about the field as it affects tax shelter investment. Therefore, the person working the site, the "operator," may be the most important human factor in the deal. What is his aim? Will he pay the costs of production if the well is found to have potential? Does he have experience? Will he take advantage of the latest development technology and the advice of scientific experts? Does he have anything at risk in the project?

Because you are a passive investor in most tax shelters, the managers you choose for your investment must be capable and trustworthy. With all the additional imponderables of oil and gas deals, it is even more important that you work with people you trust. They cannot guarantee success, but they can guarantee best efforts.

TO SUM UP...

As opposed to many other kinds of tax shelter, oil and gas offer high risks and high potential rewards. In addition, the investor must really be seeking profits; the tax benefits for unprofitable ventures are not as attractive as benefits associated with other shelters.

There are many concepts pertinent to oil and gas investment that you should understand and learn to apply to your individual tax situation. Depletion can be very useful, particularly if your deal pays off and you have other income to shelter at the same time. The deduction of intangible costs can be a substantial benefit in the first year of operation, when the deal has been properly structured and the general partner has kept a weather eye on the restrictions of the tax code. And the choice of a developmental project over an exploratory one may give you a degree of comfort about your investment, although you might choose the riskier but potentially more rewarding type of shelter deal.

Windfall-Profits Tax

If you are very fortunate, you will encounter the (financially speaking) minor annoyance of the windfall-profits tax. It applies on oil at least until mid-1994 but is not imposed on gas. The amount of the tax depends upon price-per-barrel state taxes that may apply and the fluctuating base price established by the government. It should be noted that this tax has recently been under attack from many interested parties; your general partner will certainly know about the current status of the tax and its likely effect upon your investment.

7

ODDS AND ENDS, EXOTICA AND ROMANCE

"Almost anything we can do to use the tax system to encourage capital investment and savings is good," a powerful senator said recently. Many officers of the federal government, however, disagree. As this ideological debate continues, the law and interpretations of the tax code may seesaw back and forth (within certain defined limits).

Make sure you have the latest information about the government's attitude toward any shelter that might interest you—particularly "exotic" or "romance" shelters. These kinds of deals can bring down the wrath of the IRS overnight. They can also appeal to the worst instincts of the incautious investor. As Robert Daniel Fierro has written in *Tax Shelters in Plain English,* "The firm of Exotica & Esoteric are never at a loss to come up with tax-shelter schemes of the most outrageous kind."

Any faithful reader of the business section is familiar with downright larcenous shelters involving master phonograph recordings and limited-edition graphic prints. While these particular deals have been stopped by the government, ingenious promoters are likely to invent similar ventures in future. When considering an unusual proposal, remember the ingredients of a good shelter: reasonable (not astonishing) tax benefits, moderate likelihood of eventually turning a profit, experienced and honorable management, and a lack of dangerous kickers (such as high risk of expensive recapture).

In fact, the Internal Revenue Service published in 1984 a list of nine questions that should help you determine whether a proposal for a tax shelter is actually a legitimate investment or a fraudulent scheme:

1. Do the tax benefits far outweigh the economic benefits?

2. Is this a transaction you would seriously consider, apart from the tax benefits, if you hoped to make a profit?

3. Do shelter assets really exist and, if so, are they insured for less than their purchase price?

4. Is there a nontax justification for the way profits and losses are allocated to partners?

5. Do the facts and supporting documents make economic sense? Or have there been sales and resales of the tax shelter property at ever-increasing prices?

6. Does the investment plan involve a gimmick, device, or sham to hide the economic reality of the transaction?

7. Does the promoter offer to backdate documents after the close of the year, and are you instructed to backdate checks covering your investment? (This is an example of what is called a "badge of fraud," a factor necessary to the successful prosecution of tax fraud cases. Any secret side agreements between the limited partner and the promoter of a shelter scheme might also constitute a badge of fraud.)

8. Is your debt a real debt, or are you assured by the promoter that you will never have to pay for it?

9. Does this transaction involve laundering United States source income through foreign corporations incorporated in a tax haven and owned by United States shareholders?

Both you and your tax adviser will want to consider such questions before you invest.

From a different standpoint, that of the tax counselor committed to the success of a tax-sheltered limited partnership investment, there are slightly different questions to consider as well:

1. When you consider the entire deal, is it an investment you would make if it were not sheltered? Will it make money?

2. Is the promoter represented by an established bank or brokerage firm? Association with a reputable firm is no guarantee that the deal will be successful, but it suggests that in-house experts have reviewed the offering.

3. How much money has the general partner made for investors in previous deals?

4. Is a professional tax opinion included with the offering that supports the tax claims of the promoter?

5. Can you afford the minimum investment necessary, and can you leave the money in the deal for as long as necessary?

With these two sets of questions in mind, we will look at a couple of the shelter ideas that may grow in the future.

RESEARCH AND DEVELOPMENT SHELTERS

Even as many tax preferences, speedy write-offs, and the investment tax credit were coming under attack in 1984, the treasury was still supportive of the continuation of the 25 percent tax credit for projects involving research and development. If not a sacred cow, this area of investment is nonetheless likely to receive government encouragement, in the form of tax benefits to the investor, in the foreseeable future. In the words of one government document, the aim should be to ensure that the tax credit is "targeted more effectively toward productivity-enhanced innovations" (whatever that might mean in practice). Congress will have to renew the credit or it will expire after 1985.

Generally speaking, the limited partnership of an R & D shelter finances a research project undertaken by a third party, with no guarantee that the research will turn out to be a success; in other words, there must be a risk factor or the IRS may question the deductions taken by the investors.

Ideally, the R & D shelter is structured so that the limited partners will receive the maximum deduction in the first year of the deal, perhaps even in excess of their actual cash contributions. According to the law, deductible expenses are those "research or experimental expenditures which are paid or incurred by [the investors] during the taxable year, in connection with a trade or business." Laboratory costs or the cost of obtaining a patent may be deductible, but expenses such as consumer surveys or advertising and promotion of the product being developed are not.

In addition to the substantial up-front deductions, however, an R & D tax shelter offers the potential for eventual profits that will be given capital gains treatment. Should the product prove to be patentable, the limited partnership will most likely transfer patent rights to the sponsor of the scheme in exchange for royalties paid on the basis of gross sales of the product. The sale of patents receives long-term capital gains treatment.

It is possible that the 25 percent tax credit will also be of use, but it does not apply to start-up deals and can only be used to lower your tax bill on the income you receive from the business venture.

R & D: Some Special Considerations

Someone wants your money, of course, because the product being developed in an R & D shelter probably does not yet exist, at least in marketable form, and obviously has no history in the marketplace; in other words, it is unlikely that you will be able to get any leveraging of your investment. On the other hand, if the product actually fills a need, you may do very well.

How do you know? You don't, but investment advisers believe that you can afford yourself a reasonable degree of protection. For one thing, you should seek the advice of a professional who understands the field in which your product is being developed. Ask him or her whether the idea seems feasible, given the current state of technology, and whether or not it would be useful, practical, and likely to have a long life on the marketplace. You should even find out whether the funding for the development of the product seems sufficient to the outside observer and how your third-party developers are regarded by their peers. Has there been a marketing feasibility study? Is the potential market large enough to justify the development of the product? Do larger, better-financed companies produce, or are they about to produce, a competitive product?

Most of all, you should try to make that difficult distinction between what is remarkable or innovative and what is marketable. It may well be that the entrepreneurial team funded by your limited partnership has come up with an idea that is admirable, but does the world want it? Can the world make practical use of it? And, of course, can the world afford to buy it? Many R & D shelters offered involve highly sophisticated industries, and you may succumb to the apparent brilliance of an idea without taking a hard-nosed look at its marketability. Holography, for example, is a fascinating technological achievement, but its market uses are not yet legion. Presumably, you are more interested in turning your investment into a substantial royalty income in the next few years than in subsidizing the development of an exotic product that will earn little more than the attention of science magazines.

★ To protect the actual rate of return on your tax shelter investment, be sure that your royalties will be based upon a fixed percentage of sales prices, not a fixed dollar amount. Inflation over the long term would reduce the actual value of the latter.

Here's another consideration: The IRS may take an interest in your R & D shelter. The agency may find, for example, that your shelter does not comply with the at-risk rules, particularly if the sponsor has a commitment to buy out you and your limited partners. If the limited partnership receives stock or existing technology from the sponsor, the agency may disallow a percentage of your deductions on the theory that the amount was actually a nondeductible payment for the stock or technology. In some cases the IRS might even contend that your arrangement is a joint venture between the sponsor and the limited partnership and that you and your limited partners must therefore share the R & D deductions with the sponsor. The worst scenario would be a determination by the IRS that your limited partnership is in fact merely a lender to the sponsor, providing financing, and not justified in taking the deductions.

★ If *any* kind of shelter is so obviously abusive that it reaches the attention of the IRS early on, the agency takes the "front end" approach of alerting investors that their claimed credits will probably not be allowed. In 1983, the agency sent out 11,000 such letters, also warning of an audit and possible penalty charges.

FARM SHELTERS

The shelter potential of farming ventures includes the breeding, feeding, and (when applicable) racing of livestock. Taxable income from other sources can be offset by the losses generated in such activities, and there are other advantages to investment in farm-related shelters as well. Generally speaking, financing for such ventures is fairly easy to obtain in most parts of the country. In addition, it is usually true that farmland appreciates in value over the years (though there are significant exceptions).

The most important thing to remember is that the shelter must be operated as a business, or the IRS will determine that you are actually engaged in a (nondeductible) hobby. The farming enterprise must go into the black in at least two years of a five-year cycle, or two in a seven-year cycle if livestock is involved. You should also be ready to prove that you are indeed actively engaged in the operation of the enterprise. If challenged by the IRS, you should be able to prove, for example, that you've been making improvements in the property and paying attention to basic maintenance, just as you would in any profit-oriented business. You could hire expert help or show that you've invested the same kind of attention in your farm shelter that you have invested in your regular business activities. You should be able to produce detailed records showing that you use a professional bookkeeping system, that you have kept abreast of changing economic conditions, and that you have made changes in your operation in response to those changes. Also, according to some tax experts, you should not add too many improvements that merely enhance the recreational value of the property for you and your family. In all ways you must show that the farm is primarily a business activity.

If legitimate, your farming tax shelter will give you the benefit of depreciation deductions, deductions for interest on the mortgage and for operating expenses, and a 10 percent investment tax credit. In addition, you will probably be able to receive capital gains treatment when your up-front write-offs are eventually recaptured.

Depreciation in a farm shelter can be applied to all equipment and buildings that are used in the operation and to any part of the property that produces income. The cost of livestock is depreciated over a period designated as the "useful life" of each animal; racehorses over two years old and breeding stock more than twelve years old, for example, are depreciated over a period of three years at rates, in succession, of 25 percent, 38 percent, and 37 percent. The investment tax credit is applied to your taxable income for the year in which you buy a new piece of equipment; also, operating costs are deductible in the year you pay them.

The operation of a farm is likely to be complicated and time-consuming, and it is essential, according to everyone familiar with farm shelters, that you find responsible, experienced, and resourceful help in managing your farm. Just as important, you should choose an activity that gives you pleasure; it is not a good idea to invest in a cattle feeding operation, say, if cows bore you, when you might derive a great deal of pleasure from a different activity, such as viticulture or horse racing. Remember, too, that farming is subject to the whims of nature, whims that can translate dramatically into market factors. Recently, an insect caused havoc in California agriculture, a disease shook the citrus industry in Florida. Weather can wipe out a crop, your farm laborers can strike for higher wages, and oversupply or fickle public taste (such as the sudden demise of the kiwi fruit as a fashionable upscale item) can force prices so low you won't make back your costs.

Nevertheless, if farm operations appeal to you and if you are willing to live with the risks involved and maintain close oversight, you may enjoy this type of shelter. According to current shelter statistics you will most likely be investing in either cattle feeding or cattle breeding operations.

Fattening Them Up

Feeding ventures are highly leveraged, with the limited partnership actually providing as little as 5 percent of the total cost; all or part of the loan can be nonrecourse. The purpose of the venture is to keep the animals for a few months in a feedlot, then sell them at a profit (a price higher than the original price of the cattle plus the expenses of feeding and caring for them). To a large extent, the investor is in the hands of the feedlot operator, who must plan his buy and sell activities in order to take advantage of fluctuating market prices for cattle. Bad timing can lead to financial disaster.

Check with your tax adviser to see whether the government has imposed new restrictions on the shelter that interests you. For example, it is no longer possible to deduct the cost of prepaid feed until it is consumed.

Breeding for Capital Gains

Also highly leveraged, a breeding operation offers tax deferral for a longer period than a feeding operation, and it should also produce long-term capital gains. Generally speaking, the herd will grow large enough in five to seven years for a sale to be profitable, assuming market conditions are favorable. The promoter of the shelter will find a rancher to buy, maintain, and sell the animals. Of course, this should be someone in whom you can place your confidence, since you are a passive investor. The rancher has to possess a wide variety of skills, from dealing with the day-to-day care of the herd to knowing when it is best to offer the cattle for sale.

An extra tax advantage of breeding schemes is that accelerated depreciation schedules can be used for cattle that are bought for the operation, although not for cattle that are raised by it (but if the raised cattle are kept for at least two years, your earnings from their sale will be given capital gains treatment).

MISCELLANEOUS...

Have you always wanted a share in the seemingly glamorous life of the professional sports world? Are you envious of the famous "kings" of the sport of kings, horse racing? It's possible that you can find a tax sheltered investment in professional baseball, racing, and other sports activities, but you shouldn't go near them unless you know and love the particular enterprise. As always, you must research the careers of the people with whom you would be investing money. Take a good look at the risks involved and weigh them against the expected gains.

SUMMING UP: THE TYPES OF RELIEF

At this point it might be useful to review the various tax shelters mentioned in this book, with an eye to the type of relief offered by each.

Agriculture: "Feeder cattle" schemes offer tax deferral based upon the deduction of supplies as they are consumed. "Breeder cattle" deals offer tax deferral created by depreciation and the possibility of capital gains treatment when the cattle are held for at least twenty-four months. An investment tax credit is also available.

Equipment Leasing: This type of shelter offers tax deferral and a front-end investment tax credit based upon the amount the investor has at risk. Because of accelerated depreciation, losses range from three to five years. When the lease term ends, the equipment is sold and proceeds are taxed at the investor's ordinary income tax rates.

Oil and Gas: In addition to tax deferral and income conversion, these shelters can offer limited tax credits. As we have seen, both the write-off of intangible drilling costs *and* (a percentage of) the depletion allowance create the deferral in the early years of the shelter. Tax credits are given for the purchase of drilling equipment. The ultimate sale may receive capital gains treatment, although deductions taken for intangible drilling costs will be recaptured at ordinary income tax rates.

Real Estate: As we have seen, real estate shelters provide tax deferral, conversion of taxable income into earnings that receive capital gains treatment, leverage, and in some cases, the use of tax credits. In general, the investor receives about five years or more of tax loss, after which the property is sold to produce earnings, all or part of which are capital gains.

Research and Development: The appeal of these shelters is twofold—tax deferral and conversion of income. The deferral derives from the deduction of monies expended on research; capital gains treatment will be afforded to earnings on the sale of inventories or of the process.

Which shelter is right for you? Only you, with the help of your tax adviser, lawyer, or accountant, can decide. (Any tax shelter decision should also be thoroughly discussed with your spouse, even if only one marriage partner typically makes most of the family's investment decisions. Your spouse should know how much money is being put at risk, and for how long. And, in the event of your demise, your spouse should be prepared for the decisions that will have to be made as a shelter deal draws to a close.)

In the next chapter we'll take a brief look at the likely future of the tax shelter concept.

8

THE EVER-CHANGING SHELTER

As this book was going to press, legislators, business leaders, social activists, government bureaucrats, and ordinary taxpayers were heatedly debating the structure and aims of the nation's tax system. Whatever the results of that debate, the discussion is likely to continue, and the consequences of change are likely to be felt for years to come.

Shelter activity is only one aspect of the national debate, but it does attract attention. Many Americans question the concept itself, either because they feel that the rich are being given a tax break not available to other taxpayers, or because they feel that it is not the business of government to encourage investment in any particular sector of the economy. In addition, the abuse of shelters has angered both public officials and private citizens, causing some people to suspect that the game might not be worth the candle—that is, that the cost of policing tax shelters might not be worth the social gains to be derived from the concept.

Nevertheless, tax shelters will probably be with us in the foreseeable future, if most tax analysts are correct, even if there are changes in the law and an increased determination on the part of the IRS to crack down on abusers (perhaps you have noticed that the government is eagerly publicizing its enforcement activities, evidently hoping that the publicity will deter potential abusers).

In 1984, the Treasury Department announced that the annual loss of revenue from abusive tax shelters was in the neighborhood of

$3.6 billion. It is this kind of statistic that has taxpayers, their elected officials, and the courts demanding effective enforcement. The IRS has increased the number of shelter cases it refers to the Justice Department for prosecution, and the courts have become less lenient than they were just a few years ago. According to IRS figures, 67 percent of those convicted of tax shelter abuse in 1981 were actually given prison sentences. By 1984, 87 percent of convicted offenders were sent to prison—the highest percentage for any tax-related conviction. In addition, according to the government, the average fine for abusers of tax shelters jumped over the same period from $6,000 to $20,000, while the average prison term increased from eleven to fifty-one months. At the same time, IRS auditing procedures dramatically improved. Only a few years ago, 57 percent of returns selected for audit proved incorrect as filed; today, however, 83 percent are proved incorrect as a result of improved selection methods.

Meanwhile, the IRS has stepped up activity to seek injunctions against the sale of shelters that it feels are abusive. As mentioned earlier, the agency now requires promoters to register their shelters and have available for IRS inspection a list of the investors in the deal. The investor is required to list on their personal income tax return the registration numbers of any shelters in which he or she participates.

WORTH THE HASSLE?

All this activity has made many taxpayers extremely wary about becoming involved in tax shelters. Some tax experts have grumbled that the government may be overreacting, with the side effect of discouraging honest taxpayers from reaping the tax benefits of legitimate shelter activity. Some observers have complained that a disproportionate amount of media attention was devoted to tax shelters in the reportage of the Tax Reform Act of 1984. (By the way, the act is the fifth major amendment of tax law in nine years, an indication of the complex and changing nature of the Internal Revenue Code.)

Nevertheless, the act is no doubt an accurate reflection of congressional concern about the potential for shelter abuse and may indicate the beginning of a trend. Perhaps the most indicative provision is the emphasis on the "economic performance rule," meant to correct what government officials felt was a failure in the previous law to take into account the time value of money. In effect, the rule disallows deductions until "economic performance" occurs. As of July 19, 1984, according to the act, "all of the events that establish liability for an amount, for the purpose of determining whether such amount has been incurred with respect to any item, are treated as not occurring any earlier than the time that economic performance occurs with respect to that item." The courts had interpreted earlier law to mean that one could take a full deduction in the present for an amount to be paid in the future; Congress felt that the practice overstated the time value of the expense.

Changes in Oil and Gas

Attention has been concentrated on deductions for prepayment of intangible drilling costs, particularly when this high initial write-off is created by a drilling program initiated toward the end of the year. Therefore, you should probably avoid any year-end drilling program involving leverage, because the new law limits deductible prepayments to wells on which drilling is begun within ninety days of the end of the year in which you claim the deduction. Clearly, the sponsor of your limited partnership must have substantial control over the actual operations in the field to ensure that this proviso is taken into account, particularly if the shelter deal has been put together in the third or fourth quarter of the year. The amount of deduction attributable to partnership borrowing or partnership-facilitated debt is also limited now to the amount of drilling actually performed in the year of the deduction; thus, the benefits you would formerly have received in leveraged oil and gas programs are reduced.

The act does not change one basic truth about such programs, however: you should not be dazzled by the untrustworthy promise of multiple write-offs, and you should look at the potential of the program for competitive economic performance.

Changes in Real Estate

As already noted, the 1984 act stretches the depreciation period for most properties from fifteen to eighteen years, with the exception of low-income housing; the effect is to reduce the amount of tax deductions attributable to depreciation in any one year. The act also curtails prepayment of interest and other expenses, which will affect some real estate syndications that have previously used prepaid interest expenses to inflate first-year deductions. Now there are also limitations on the use of the accrual method of accounting to increase tax benefits offered by a real estate shelter. Accrued expenses are no longer legitimately deductible for tax purposes until there is actual payment, or "economic performance." There are also new limitations on allocation of income and deductions to limited partners who join a cash-basis limited partnership after such items have accrued.

It seems likely that these changes in the law will make real estate shelters less attractive to certain types of investors. Promoters may respond to these changes by paying less for properties; they may try to compensate for the reduced tax benefits by increasing leverage. Increased leverage, however, greatly increases investor risk even as it increases the ratio of tax deductions to actual cash investment in the deal. Tax analysts strongly advise that you be wary of real estate deals that emphasize write-offs rather than the fundamental profit motive, particularly by means of inflated interest deductions or purchase prices or through the use of interest payments that do not actually affect cash flow.

Changes in Equipment Leasing

The front-end investment tax credit may be affected by the 1984 changes, and tax benefits have been restricted on shelters that lease equipment to tax-exempt organizations and governmental agencies. You and your tax adviser should discuss changes in the real estate provisions and present value concepts, then evaluate the possible impact these changes may have on any equipment leasing shelter.

These revisions in tax law are designed to emphasize the original intent of tax shelters: to encourage taxpayers to become involved in legitimate, well-structured deals that legally take advantage of tax incentives.

The 1984 act was also written to underscore the government's intention to accept as legitimate only those investments that have a true business purpose. You should be looking for investment performance and capital preservation; you should not be looking for excessive leverage or inflated tax deductions, nor should you be bringing the integrity of your intentions into question by waiting until near the end of the year to invest in a shelter.

THE FINAL DECISION: YOU'RE ON YOUR OWN

We've said that a tax shelter might not be right for many taxpayers; for others, despite all the caution that is necessary, a shelter can be a very important, beneficial part of an investment portfolio. The IRS crackdown on abusive shelters should not scare the investor away from legitimate shelter activities; neither should the risks involved in some types of shelter frighten the investor away from those that are structured to offer reasonable chance of long-term gains for a minimum amount of short-term risk. If you are in the 50 percent tax bracket (or perhaps somewhat lower than that), and if you are able to tie up money in a shelter for the time period necessary, you may well find that a tax shelter is a conservative, sensible investment option.

Let's review those elements of a tax shelter that must match up with your own tax situation. There are four possible kinds of benefit:

1. **Tax deferral**—tax losses are deducted from current income, as in the case of deductions for accelerated depreciation; or tax liability is deferred by having income deferred. In effect, the government makes an interest-free loan available to the investor by means of this tax-saving device.

2. **Conversion**—your current income is converted by the shelter into long-term capital gains, thus earning favorable tax treatment at rates lower than ordinary income tax rates. In the short term, as we have seen, ordinary income is offset by the deductions generated by the shelter.

3. **Leverage**—write-offs are generated by the debt, since depreciation deductions are based, not upon the actual cash invested, but upon the total purchase price. (Only in real estate shelters can the debt be nonrecourse.)

4. **Tax credits**—by reducing the amount of taxes you owe on a dollar-for-dollar basis, tax credits in effect reduce the costs of a shelter's assets (which, of course, increase its attractiveness). These credits are allowed in addition to deductions, but the depreciable basis of the property must be reduced by 50 percent of the investment tax credit (for example, by 5 percent if the up-front credit is 10 percent).

★ The present depreciation method, the accelerated cost recovery system, may be changed soon, if proposals from the Treasury are adopted. The proposed real cost recovery system would allow recovery of the inflation-adjusted cost of a business asset rather than only the original cost; in addition, the write-offs during the recovery period would be uniform each year. Currently, business assets are placed in one of five categories, written off in from three to eighteen years; the proposed changes would place assets in one of seven categories, to be written off in from five to sixty-three years. If these changes are in fact approved, they may have some effect on your investment strategy.

SOME QUESTIONS FOR YOUR CHECKLIST

Here's a quick round-up of factors you should consider before making a final decision.

Don't Go Overboard on Leveraging

Remember that the annual deduction allowed on your income tax return for interest expense is usually restricted to $10,000 plus "net investment income." If you are borrowing money to finance your investment in a tax shelter, be certain you will not come into conflict with IRS restrictions on interest.

Is the Profit Motive Paramount?

When reading the prospectus for a shelter, do you get the feeling that the promoters are trying to lure only those investors who want excessive tax benefits, or are they describing, with appropriate sobriety, a deal that has been designed to gain genuine economic benefits?

Who Are These People?

The advantage of having a reliable, experienced general partner is obvious; he or she has the same relationship to your deal as the CEO has to a company, with fewer restrictions on the freedom to act and make decisions.

The "Entity of Choice"

Usually, you will want to participate in a limited partnership and should make sure that your shelter is operated in that form. It is possible that a general partnership, joint venture, regular corporation, or subchapter-S corporation might have advantages for your own situation, however; this is a matter to be discussed with your tax adviser.

Avoid Gray Areas

By now you are well aware that this book has been written with the firm conviction that an investor is best advised to become involved only in deals that are legitimate in black-and-white terms. You should work only with promoters, general partners, or tax consultants who share a belief that exploitation of the gray areas of the law, the loopholes, is likely to bring an audit and a determination from the IRS that fraud is being attempted. Sharp practices in regard to tax law do not pay off; eschew the company of those who would convince you otherwise.

Don't Exceed the At-Risk Limitation

Remember: Your losses are limited by the amount of money or other properties you have at risk in a shelter, and both the at-risk amount and the projected basis of a shelter are annually adjusted, thereby affecting your tax situation.

Be Wary of Phantoms

As we have seen, a danger of some shelters is the sudden appearance of "phantom" income—a paper income that, though nonexistent, nevertheless generates an actual tax liability. Timing is important, as is the type of income the shelter is structured to generate.

Avoid the Alternative Minimum Tax

The cruel irony of triggering the alternative minimum tax by investment in a tax shelter can be avoided by careful tax planning; set your tax adviser to work on this one.

Have Special Allocations Explained

Unless the investor is a skilled accountant, the "special allocations" of a deal may be very difficult to understand—perhaps purposely so. Your tax consultant should be asked to explain any such allocations to your satisfaction and should help you understand the long-term implications.

Beware of "Audit Bait"

As noted on page 38, the IRS is likely to audit tax shelter deals that have certain questionable characteristics. In addition, your tax adviser should be aware of the kinds of shelter that have been attacked by the agency in the past (not all are as obvious as deals in oyster farming, classic automobiles, and greyhound racing, which in the past have furnished good copy to the financial press).

WHEN ALL IS SAID AND DONE

This book has been intended as a very general introduction to a complex, constantly changing topic. If you decide that a tax shelter is not the appropriate investment for you at the present time, you might still benefit from the tax-saving plans described in the first two chapters of the book. If you decide that you would like to invest in a shelter deal, do your homework and keep abreast of developments in tax law and government as well as court interpretations of the law. You should also get the best professional advice available to you.

Above all, remember: A tax shelter is an investment, not a scam, and should have as its aim an eventual return of real dollars. Perhaps the very word "shelter" has contributed to so much misunderstanding of the real aim of the laws involving tax shelters. The mechanism may better be described as "enhanced investment" or "income conversion." In any event, do your best to understand the government's intentions with regard to encouraging this form of investment—to ensure that you and your partners are operating within the framework of those intentions.